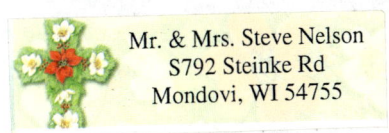

The Wine of Roman Babylon

View of the inside of St. Peter's Basilica in Rome, showing the gaudy splendor and decadence of the ruler of Roman Babylon, who professes to be the successor of the humble apostle of Jesus Christ.

The Wine of Roman Babylon

By
Mary E. Walsh

TEACH Services, Inc.
New York

**PRINTED IN
THE UNITED STATES OF AMERICA**
World rights reserved. This book or any portion thereof may not be copied or reproduced in any form or manner whatever, except as provided by law, without the written permission of the publisher, except by a reviewer who may quote brief passages in a review.

The author assumes full responsibility for the accuracy of all facts and quotations as cited in this book.

2005 06 07 08 09 10 11 12 · 5 4 3 2 1

Copyright © 1945 The Southern Publishing Association
Copyright © 2001, 2005 TEACH Services, Inc.
ISBN-13: 978-1-57258-204-9
ISBN-10: 1-57258-204-9
Library of Congress Control Number: 2001091814

Published by

TEACH Services, Inc.
www.TEACHServices.com

THE AUTHOR

Mary E. Walsh, the author of this book "The Wine of Roman Babylon," was born in a Roman Catholic family in Ireland. Her forbears for many generations back were confirmed believers in the doctrines of the papacy. Baptized into the Roman Church when only one day old, she continued a faithful communicant of that religious body for 20 years. Then becoming interested in reading the Sacred Scriptures, she was led by her study to renounce the papal faith. Thereafter devoting her energies to the propagation of the evangelical doctrines found in Holy Writ, she has had many years of success in teaching the gospel truths to others. At present she is serving as a Bible instructor in evangelical work in the United States.

This book does not propose to delve into the abstruse, philosophical discussions by the notable theologians of the Roman Catholic Church, but rather presents a candid and practical study of the principal papal doctrines as they are taught to the rank and file of that sect.

CONTENTS

1. Babylon the Great 1
2. Tradition 11
3. Infant Baptism 19
4. Auricular Confession 31
5. Penance 39
6. The Mass 45
7. Omission of the Cup 59
8. Masses and Purgatory 63
9. Peter and the Rock 73
10. Peter and the Keys 83
11. The Immaculate Conception 105
12. Invocation of the Saints 119
13. Immortality of the Soul 141
14. Eternal Torment in Hell 147
15. Extreme Unction 157
16. Sunday Observance 165
17. Appendices 181
Bibliography 233

St. Peter's, situated in front of the Vatican in Rome, is the most noted of Roman Catholic churches. It probably is visited by more people than any other temple on earth. The papal system which centers there was the dominant political and religious institution in the world during the Dark Ages. (Photo by Wide World.)

CHAPTER I

Babylon the Great

IN THE Holy Scriptures there are revealed two churches—the true and the counterfeit—which are diametrically opposed to each other. God gives the title "synagogue of Satan" [Rev. 3:9] to the false or apostate church. It is Satan's masterpiece of counterfeiting the true church. He has a wonderful organization and a large membership.

Satan's counterfeit religious system, which he uses to deceive the whole world, lacks nothing to make it complete and like the genuine. His ministers "are false apostles, deceitful workers, transforming themselves into the apostles of Christ. And no marvel; for Satan himself is transformed into an angel of light. Therefore it is no great thing if his ministers also be transformed as the ministers of righteousness." [2 Cor. 11:13-15]

It is by the mingling of false teachings with truth that this counterfeit church has been promoted. God's true church, in contrast, will not seek that which does not bear His mark and superscription. Christ Himself declared that worship which mingles the human with the divine is worthless, and foretold the fate of the counterfeit religious system of doctrines and institutions. "In vain they do worship Me, teaching for doctrines the commandments of men...Every plant, which My heavenly Father hath not planted, shall be rooted up." [Matt. 15:9, 13]

Since man-made worship is vain or worthless, because it is counterfeit, we must have some standard by which to test doctrines and determine what is truth. This test is given in the Holy Bible: "To the law and to the testimony: if they speak not according to this word, it is because there is no light in them." [Isa. 8:20]

It is quite natural for men to desire to belong to the true church. But with the multiplicity of sects, with their conflicting creeds and doctrines, it may seem difficult to determine which is the true one. It is not very difficult after all. God's word declares that the two outstanding characteristics of the true church in the last days, marks which distinguish her from all others, are keeping the commandments of God and having the testimony of Jesus, which is the Spirit of prophecy. [Rev. 12:17; 19:10]

As foretold in prophecy, [Rev. 12] Satan's rage against Christ, whom he failed to hold in the tomb, is hurled against His followers, whom he has persecuted bitterly down through the centuries to the remnant living in the time of Christ's return. The final outburst of Satanic wrath will be against the individuals "which keep the commandments of God, and have the testimony of Jesus Christ." [Rev. 12:17] But though Satan wars against those who obey the law of God, we are not left in doubt as to the result of the issue. The Lord will vindicate His law, and at His coming He will utter these words: "Here is the patience of the saints: here are they that keep the commandments of God, and the faith of Jesus." [Rev. 14:12]

Thus God has a true church in the world, and Satan also has his, and there is constant war between them. Our position in this conflict depends on our attitude toward God and the truth that He has revealed to men, for all other worship is "vain" and will be "rooted up." [Matt. 15:9, 13] According to the standard set up by God, the true church makes the "commandments of God" and "the faith of Jesus" [Rev. 14:12; Isa. 8:20] the very foundation of its teachings. Because the false church is a close counterfeit of the true, we would not expect to find the false system repudiating the *whole* law of God. Satan's system deals in "the knowledge of good and evil." [Gen. 2:17] It rejects a part of the Ten Commandments, substituting for a command of God a precept of man. It is this perversion of worship that has given rise to numerous sects and creeds. Our individual attitude to the law of God determines the church to which we belong.

The wrath of "the dragon," Satan, is said to be directed against "the woman." [Rev. 12:1-3, 17] A woman is thus used in symbolic prophecy to represent a church. In the Revelation we have the true and the false church each symbolized by a woman. John saw "a woman clothed with the sun, and the moon under her feet, and upon her head a crown of twelve stars; and she being with child cried, travailing in birth, and pained to be delivered." [Rev. 12:1-3, 17] This glorious woman is the true church of Christ. "I have likened the daughter of Zion to a comely and delicate woman." [Jer. 6:2] "I am jealous over you with godly jealousy: for I have espoused you to one husband, that I may present you as a chaste virgin to Christ." [2 Cor. 11:2] Her child is the Lord Jesus Christ, born in Bethlehem and "caught up unto God" after His death and resurrection. [Acts 1:9-11] The sun with which the woman is clothed represents the full light of truth shining from the Bible after the first advent of Christ. The moon represents the gospel light of truth as reflected by the symbolic, sacrificial service of the Old Testament, which pointed to Christ and was thus illuminated with borrowed meaning, just as the lunar orb shines with borrowed light from the solar body.

In Revelation 17 is God's picture of the false church. The symbol used for it is also a woman, a lewd and fallen one. It is pictured thus: "There came one of the seven angels which had the seven vials, and talked with me, saying unto me, Come hither; I will show unto thee the judgment of the

The Wine of Roman Babylon

great whore that sitteth upon many waters." [Rev. 17:1] So clearly does God prophetically portray this apostate religious power which would bring multitudes to ruin, that no room is left for doubt as to the identity of the false system of worship to which He refers.

The church referred to in the prophecy would hold universal sway, for she is "the great whore that sitteth upon many waters." We have the following definition of the waters as a prophetic symbol: "The waters which thou sawest, where the whore sitteth, are peoples, and multitudes, and nations, and tongues." [Rev. 17:15] This shows that many nations would be under the domination of this apostate religious power. History attests to the fulfillment of this prophetic utterance, as seen in the position occupied for centuries by the Roman Catholic Church, when kings and their subjects alike bowed to her commands.

She was foreseen by the prophet in the symbol of the vile and wicked woman who would "sit upon a scarlet-colored beast." A beast in symbolic prophecy represents a political power. [Dan. 7:17, 23; 8:20, 21] Through the mingling of pagan and Christian doctrines in the early centuries, and the union of church and state from the time of Constantine I to Justinian's reign, was brought about the pontifical eminence and regal authority of the false system that is portrayed in the prophecy.

She is described as one "with whom the kings of the earth have committed fornication." [Rev. 17:2] These words refer to the illicit union between the kings of the earth and the formidable, corrupt, and apostate church. The condition that led to her fornication, or whoredom, was a betrayal of her sacred vow to be true to her real husband, Jesus Christ, who is "the Head of the church." [Eph. 5:23]

It requires humility to be a follower of the meek and lowly One. [Matt. 10:38; Luke 14:26, 27] But this church became weary of her self-denial, and went after other lovers, who would give her the material things of life: dress, tables of luxury, social standing, political eminence, and finally the highest position—that of a crowned queen with a royal throne. [Rev. 17:2, 18; 18:3] Her course has been like that of Israel of old. "For their [the Israelites'] mother hath played the harlot: she that conceived them hath done shamefully: for she said, I will go after my lovers, that give me my bread and my water, my wool and my flax, mine oil and my drink." [Hos. 2:5] "Shall not that land be greatly polluted? But thou hast played the harlot with many lovers; yet return again to Me, saith the Lord. Lift up thine eyes unto the high places, and see where thou hast not been lien with. In the ways hast thou sat for them, as the Arabian in the wilderness; and thou hast polluted the land with thy whoredoms and thy wickedness. Therefore the showers have been withholden, and there hath been no latter rain; and thou hadst a whore's forehead, thou refusedst to be ashamed." [Jer. 3:1-3]

Thus the church would court the friendship of the world, dishonor her Lord, with a resulting spiritual declension and drought. The showers of the Holy Spirit could not be poured out during the Dark Ages because of unfaithfulness to the law and the word of God.

"And I saw a woman sit upon a scarlet-colored beast, full of names of blasphemy." [Rev. 17:3, 18] According to this prophecy, the woman's mounting the beast indicates the pre-eminence which the apostate church would hold in civil affairs, as queen over the kings of the earth. The names of blasphemy referred to show the aspirations of the leader of the church in assuming the prerogatives of God.

Two ways of blaspheming, according to the Bible are these: (1) by claiming the power to forgive sins; and (2) by laying claim to be the Son of God. Christ was accused by the Pharisees of blasphemy when He forgave sin. "And when He saw their faith, He said unto him, Man, thy sins are forgiven thee. And the scribes and the Pharisees began to reason, saying, Who is this which speaketh blasphemies? Who can forgive sins, but God alone?" [Luke 5:20, 21] Christ would have been guilty of blasphemy in claiming to forgive sins, if He had been a mere man, for God has never given that exclusive right to any human being.

The Roman Catholic Church claims that the power of absolution is invested in her priests:

"Seek where you will, through heaven and earth, and you will find but one created being who can forgive the sinner, who can free him from the chains of hell, that extraordinary being is the priest, the [Roman] Catholic priest. 'Who can forgive sins except God?' was the question which the Pharisees sneeringly asked. 'Who can forgive sins?' is the question which the Pharisees of the present day also ask, and I answer there is a man on earth that can forgive sins and that man is the [Roman] Catholic priest. Yes, beloved brethren, the priest not only declares that the sinner is forgiven, but he *really forgives him*. The priest raises his hand, he pronounces the word of absolution, and in an instant, quick as a flash of light, the chains of hell are burst asunder, and the sinner becomes a child of God. So great is the power of the priest that the judgments of heaven itself are subject to his decision."[1]

When the priest raises his hand over the penitent and pronounces the words of absolution, "I absolve thee," he is guilty of blasphemy.

Another Bible definition of blasphemy is seen in the case where the high priest asked Christ if He were the Son of God. "The high priest asked Him, and said unto Him, Art Thou the Christ, the Son of the Blessed? And Jesus said, I am: and ye shall see the Son of man sitting on the right hand of power, and coming in the clouds of heaven. Then

---

[1] Michael Muller, *The Catholic Priest* (Baltimore: Kreuzer Brothers, 1876) 78–79.

the high priest rent his clothes, and saith, What need we any further witnesses? Ye have heard the blasphemy: what think ye? And they all condemned Him to be guilty of death." [Mark 14:61-64]

Had Jesus not been the Son of God, as He said He was, the charge of blasphemy made against Him by the high priest would have been true. Who of the human family have claimed a right to the title, "Son of God," or "Another Christ"? A Romanist says:

"'Thou art a priest forever,' says the ordaining bishop, 'set apart to offer up gifts and sacrifices for sins' (Hebrews 5). As he lays his hands on the bowed head before him, the eternal Spirit stamps the soul of the priest with His mysterious 'mark' or 'character.'

"The Jewish priests of the old law wore always on their foreheads a silver plate bearing the words: *Sanctum Domino*—'Holy to the Lord'; the ministers of God's church carry graven on their souls the sign of ordination, which can never be effaced. In the eyes of God and His heavenly court he is no longer a man, a sinful child of Adam, but an *alter Christus*, 'another Christ.'

"'Did I meet an angel and a priest,' said St. Francis of Assisi, 'I would salute the priest before the angel.'

"'Thou art a priest forever,' is written on his soul. Forever a priest of the Most High with power over the Almighty.

"Forever, whether a saint on earth or buried in sin, whether glorious in heaven or burning in hell, 'marked and sealed and signed' as God's most precious treasure which no earthly hand may touch."[2]

When holy orders are conferred upon the priest, and he assumes the title of *alter Christus* (another Christ), it is then that the guilt of blasphemy is registered against him and those who ordain him.

---

[2] Wm. Doyle, S. J., *Shall I Be a Priest?*, 16th ed. (Dublin: Office of the Irish Messenger) 8.

The Wine of Roman Babylon

Thus this church, through her priesthood, fits into the prophetic picture. When a religious system elevates men to the position held by Christ, it is time for its adherents to search God's word earnestly and prayerfully. What antecedes the exaltation of the human is the discarding of Bible truth and the adoption of man-made doctrines. The great apostasy originally began with those "who changed the truth Of God into a lie, and worshiped and served the creature more than the Creator." [Rom. 1:25] The apostle Paul, under divine inspiration, foretold the coming of the antichrist whose aspirations would presume to transcend the realms of this earth to the supernatural. lie spoke prophetically of one "who opposeth and exalteth himself above all that is called God, or that is worshiped; so that he as God sitteth in the temple of God, showing himself that he is God." [2 Thess. 2:4] How it must grieve Heaven to see a church making such a high profession and yet being averse to the teachings of the Divine Word!

Since dress plays an important part in the social circle of the world, the apostate church, courting the friendship of earthly potentates, exchanged the simple white linen of the righteousness of Christ [Rev. 19:8] for the gaudy, rich robes of the world, thus enhancing her standing among the kings of the earth. "And the woman was arrayed in purple and scarlet color, and decked with gold and precious stones and pearls, having a golden cup in her hand full of abominations and filthiness of her fornication." [Rev. 17:4]

Purple, a token of royalty [Dan. 5:7, margin; Matt. 27:28], shows that this apostate church would associate with the kings of the earth. At certain feasts of the church, the vestments which the priests wear are purple. Those who compose the college of cardinals dress in scarlet. Scarlet is also a symbol of sin, which is the transgression of God's law. "Come now, and let us reason together, saith the Lord: though your sins be as scarlet, they shall be as white as snow; though they be red like crimson, they shall be as wool." [Isa. 1:18; 1 John 3:4.]

She is described as being "decked with gold" — margin, "gilded" — having a beautiful outward appearance, while her interior is nothing but base metal. The characteristic of gold is to be seen in the true church of God. [Rev. 3:18] But here is a church gilded over. At heart it is base, vile, and corrupt. She is also "decked with...precious stones and pearls," ornaments that are worn by those who love ostentation. "Love makes no parade, gives itself no airs."[3]

When a church or an individual bedecks and goes out to attract the attention of the world, it is a sure sign that the simplicity of the meek and lowly Christ has been lost. The less a person has on the inside, the more he puts on the outside. If this fallen church were to don the simple attire of the true body of Christ, she would no longer go arm in arm with the potentates of the earth. We never read of Jesus or the apostles courting the favor of the Caesars of Rome. The humble Galilean garb which they wore never would have commended them to a royal court.

Here, too, is a church whose language and customs are in keeping with court life. The diplomatic relationships which this church had during the Dark Ages, and which have recently been restored, cause its head, the pope, and his legates to feel perfectly at home as they negotiate with the civil rulers of earth. Christ and His followers were not politicians, and were they on earth, royal palaces would be strange places to them.

The examination of the "cup" which is in the band of the woman next demands attention. This is the most significant detail of the prophetic symbol, for the Holy Word declares: "The inhabitants of the earth have been made drunk with the wine of her fornication." [Rev. 17:2] It is evident that all the glory and splendid appearance of the

---

[3] 1 Cor. 13:5, Moffatt.

The Wine of Roman Babylon

counterfeit church are but a lure to attract men to taste the intoxicating and deadly potion found in this cup. Words cannot too strongly state the importance of every person's need of knowing exactly what is this wine in Babylon's cup. To the exposition of this part of the prophetic symbol the remainder of this book is devoted. As everything about the false church is a counterfeit of some feature of the true church, so the wine she offers is the substitute for the pure water of life flowing from the living fountain of the Sacred Word of God. [John 6:63; Jer. 2:13] In order to recognize the poison in the wine of her cup, we must make use of the test established by God: "To the law and to the testimony: if they speak not according to this word, it is because there is no light in them." [Isa. 8:20] Therefore let us compare the doctrines of the papal church, as taught in original sources, and in authorized Roman Catholic catechisms and doctrinal books, with the true teachings revealed by God in the Holy Scriptures.

Also see Appendix p. 183.

CHAPTER II

Tradition

WE SHALL designate the first sip from the cup of Roman Babylon as "Tradition." The following quotations clearly set before us the position of the Roman Catholic Church concerning the Holy Bible:

"A rule of faith, or a competent guide to heaven, must be able to instruct in all the truths necessary for salvation. Now the Scriptures alone do not contain all the truths which a Christian is bound to believe, nor do they explicitly enjoin all the duties which he is obliged to practice."[4]

Has an all-wise God failed to give us a complete guide, so that we are obliged to resort to man-made doctrines? The great apostle Paul, writing under inspiration, is very explicit on this question: "All Scripture is given by inspiration of God, and is profitable for doctrine, for reproof, for correction, for instruction in righteousness: that the man of God may be perfect, throughly furnished unto all good works." [2 Tim. 3:16, 17]

But we read in Cardinal Gibbon's popular work:

"We must, therefore, conclude that the Scriptures alone can not be a sufficient guide and rule of faith,...because they are not of themselves clear and intelligible even in matters of the highest importance, and because they do not contain all the truths necessary for salvation."[5]

---

[4] Cardinal James Gibbons, *The Faith of Our Fathers*, 110th rev. ed. (Baltimore: John Murphy Co.) 89, 90.
[5] Ibid.

This is an insult to the intelligence of God, charging Him with giving us a book that is an unintelligible and incompetent guide. One text from the Sacred Scriptures will be sufficient to set forth Heaven's position on this matter. The apostle Paul, in writing to Timothy, said: "From a child thou hast known the Holy Scriptures, which are able to make thee wise unto salvation through faith which is in Christ Jesus." [2 Tim. 3:15] If the Holy Scriptures are such an unintelligible book, how could Timothy from a child grasp the plan of salvation from their study?

The importance and value of Bible study is repeatedly emphasized in the Sacred Scriptures. David declared that young people ought to study the Sacred Word. "Wherewithal shall a young man cleanse his way? By taking heed thereto according to Thy word," writes he. And he adds: "Thy word have I hid in mine heart, that I might not sin against Thee." Thus the study of the Bible is an aid to overcoming evil in a person's life. "Thy word is a lamp unto my feet, and a light unto my path." Moreover, the psalmist says: "The entrance of Thy words giveth light; it giveth understanding unto the simple." [Ps. 119:9, 11, 105, 130]

The apostle Paul commended the brethren of Berea because they tested all his teaching by the Holy Scriptures. "These were more noble than those in Thessalonica, in that they received the word with all readiness of mind, and searched the Scriptures daily, whether those things were so." [Acts 17:11]

It is true, as Roman Catholics sometimes allege, that all that Christ did and said has not been recorded in the Good Book. John says that in these words: "And there are also many other things which Jesus did, the which, if they should be written every one, I suppose that even the world itself could not contain the books that should be written." [John 21:25] Nevertheless, the apostle makes it very clear and definite that *what has been written is sufficient for our salvation* if we will believe it: "And many other signs truly did Jesus in the presence of His disciples, which are not written in this book: but these are written, that ye might believe that Jesus is the Christ, the Son of God; and that believing ye might have life through His name." [John 20:30, 31]

In stating what constitutes the armor of the Christian for fighting the battle of life against the powers of darkness, Paul says to him: "Take the helmet of salvation, and the sword of the Spirit, which is the word of God." [Ephesians 6:17] And we are assured that "the word of God is quick, and powerful, and sharper than any two-edged sword." [Heb. 4:12]

Isaiah was inspired by the Holy Spirit to say: "To the law and to the testimony: if they speak not according to this word, it is because there is no light in them." [Isa. 8:20] Thus the Sacred Word is the touchstone by which all doctrine is to be tested.

The Roman Catholic Church claims that the Holy Bible is not a competent guide. What have her leaders given to supply what they claim the Holy Scriptures lack? The following statement says it is oral tradition:

> "Some of the truths which God has revealed and which have always been taught by the [Roman] Catholic Church, are not contained in the Bible. These truths have come down to us by what is called oral tradition; that is, they have been handed down by word of mouth."[6]

Back in the days of Christ there were religious teachers who extolled the oral traditions of the elders above the written word of God. The battle was waged then between the commandments of God and the precepts of men (or oral tradition), just as the Roman Catholic Church minimizes Holy Writ and extols the traditions of the so-called "fathers

---

6 Francis J. Butler, *Holy Family Catechism*, No. 3 (Boston: Thomas J. Flynn & Co., 1904) 63.

The Wine of Roman Babylon

of the church" today. The Great Master Teacher protested strongly against oral tradition that is contrary to the Sacred Scriptures, and stated that those who teach and accept man-made doctrines, as the foundation for their belief, will find that their worship has been in vain. "He answered and said unto them, Why do ye also transgress the commandment of God by your tradition? For God commanded, saying, Honor thy father and mother: and, He that curseth father or mother, let him die the death. But ye say, Whosoever shall say to his father or his mother, It is a gift, by whatsoever thou mightest be profited by Me; and honor not his father or his mother, he shall be free. Thus have ye made the commandment of God of none effect by your tradition....But in vain they do worship Me, teaching for doctrines the commandments of men." [Matt. 15:3-6, 9]

If the papacy's position that we need oral tradition as an appendix to the Bible is correct, then the Son of God failed in teaching a complete truth, for His only textbook was the Old Testament. To vindicate the Saviour's position on this important matter, the following texts are sufficient: "And beginning at Moses and all the prophets, He expounded unto them in all the Scriptures the things concerning Himself....And He said unto them, These are the words which I spake unto you, while I was yet with you, that all things must be fulfilled, which were written in the law of Moses, and in the prophets, and in the psalms, concerning-Me." [Luke 24:27, 44]

We do not find that Jesus has changed His teaching on this important matter. In the Epistle to the Hebrews we are told that "Jesus Christ [is] the same yesterday, and today, and forever." [Heb.13:8]

The Sacred Scriptures are God's communication to man, and it is through this medium that the great principles underlying His kingdom are revealed, One would never know what truth is were it not for the Inspired Word. Its

Tradition

precepts and statutes should be as frontlets between our eyes, and as signs upon our hands. "And these words, which I command thee this day, shall be in thine heart: and thou shalt teach them diligently unto thy children, and shalt talk of them when thou sittest in thine house, and when thou walkest by the way, and when thou liest down, and when thou risest up. And thou shalt bind them for a sign upon thine hand, and they shall be as frontlets between thine eyes. And thou shalt write them upon the posts of thy house, and on thy gates." [Deut. 6:6-9]

The condition of the religious world today is alarming. The undermining of faith in the Sacred Bible by religious teachers, and the insidious remarks made about God's Ten Commandments, have resulted in a lack of reverence, in an appalling increase of infidelity, and in a growing disregard of law and order which results in criminality. Current events testify to the outcome of such teaching, and the world is rapidly ripening for the judgments of God to be poured out. All of this is because of the modern attitude toward the Divine Writings.

The true knowledge of Jesus Christ and of the plan of redemption can be obtained only through the study of the Holy Scriptures. Without this knowledge man's education avails nothing. It is character building that ought to absorb our time and attention in this life. The life is transformed by beholding the beauty of the character of Jesus Christ as revealed in the Sacred Tome. The solidity of Christ's character, and the principles which He enunciated and practiced, were the result of His adherence to the Inspired Word.

When assailed by the enemy, although weak and emaciated by hunger, the Son of God clung with a tenacity stronger than death to Holy Writ. "And Jesus...was led by the Spirit into the wilderness, being forty days tempted of the devil. And in those days He did eat nothing: and when they were ended, He afterward hungered. And the devil said unto Him, If Thou be the Son of God, command this stone that it be made bread. And Jesus answered him, saying, It is written, That man shall not live by bread alone, but by every word of God." [Luke 4:1-4]

How can weak man today meet the enemy without the Written Word? The devil knows the limitation of his power and his strength in his work in overcoming man. He knows that it is "the sword of the Spirit, which is the word of God," [Eph. 6:17; Heb. 4:12] which alone can defeat him. Therefore, he has left nothing undone either to banish from the earth God's written word or to destroy faith in it.

When the devil presented the world in its most attractive and alluring aspect to the Son of God, he met with defeat when Christ gave him an answer from what was written centuries before. "And the devil said unto Him, All this power will I give Thee, and the glory of them: for that is delivered unto me; and to whomsoever I will I give it. If Thou therefore wilt worship me, all shall be Thine. And Jesus answered and said unto him, Get thee behind Me, Satan: for it is written, Thou shalt worship the Lord thy God, and Him only shalt thou serve." [Luke 4:6-8]

Satan, seeing that Christ adhered strictly to Holy Writ's "Thus saith the Lord," then digressed from his ordinary procedure of attack. After placing Jesus on a pinnacle of the temple, he met Him with His own weapon by quoting a promise of Psalm 91:11, 12, thus showing that he, too, was familiar with the Holy Bible. When Satan repeated the promise, "Cast Thyself down from hence: for it is written, He shall give His angels charge over thee, to keep thee: and in their hands they shall bear thee up, lest at any time thou dash thy foot against a stone," [Luke 4:9, 10, 11] he omitted the very words expressing the purpose for which the promise was made. Christ, being a student of the

Tradition

Scriptures, surely detected the omission of the important words, "To keep thee in all thy ways." [Ps. 91:11]

Satan has succeeded in dividing apostate Christendom into two main classes: (1) those who deny the inspiration of the Written Word and prohibit its study; and (2) those who accept the Holy Book as the foundation of all true doctrine, but misapply and misconstrue its plainest teachings. This is one of the most dangerous and insidious snares the devil has ever set for the complete loss of souls. Peter mentions a class of people who wrested the Holy Scriptures to their own destruction. [2 Pet. 3:16] Paul also admonishes us not to handle the word of God deceitfully. [2 Cor. 4:2] [7]

The fiercest temptations came to Christ at the time of His greatest weakness, and so it will be with us. It is when human strength is diminished and everything looks dark before our vision that we must cling to the Holy Writings and repose in their promises. In man's own strength it is impossible to withstand the onslaught of the devil, but God has given to us the most effective weapon ever used in this spiritual warfare, and by it we can overcome the enemy. "For the weapons of our warfare are...mighty through God to the pulling down of strongholds; casting down imaginations, and every high thing that exalteth itself against the knowledge of God, and bringing into captivity every thought to the obedience of Christ." [2 Cor. 10:4, 5]

Thus it was by the use of the Holy Scriptures that Christ met the three great temptations which so easily overcome men today — appetite, love of the world, and presumption. How thankful we should be to have the help of the Holy Word against the enemy!

---

[7] Also see appendix, p. 187.

The Grotto of Lourdes, France, with its image of Mary, the mother of Jesus, attracts many thousands of people. Those shown in the picture are a part of the throng of 150,000 on a pilgrimage to the place. In the background can be seen many crutches hung up in testimony to miracles alleged to have been performed at the shrine. (Photo by International News.)

CHAPTER III

Infant Baptism

THE SECOND sip from Babylon's cup we shall call "Infant Baptism." This was the rite by which I was led into the Roman Catholic Church, and was made a member of that body without my consent or approval. Although it was an imposing ceremony, I do not recall anything connected with it, for I was but a day old when this rite was administered to me. I do not remember the priest's placing a white cloth on my head as he uttered the words: "Receive this white garment, and see thou carry it without stain before the judgment seat of our Lord Jesus Christ, that thou mayest have eternal life." Neither do I remember when he placed a lighted candle in my hand, signifying that I was to shine by a virtuous life before the whole world. Nor do I recall the priest's breathing three times in my face, to signify the new and spiritual life I was supposed to receive by the grace of the Holy Ghost; nor his making the sign of the cross upon my forehead and upon my breast, and at the same time sprinkling the "holy water" upon me, denoting the doctrine of my crucified Redeemer, which I was to carry in my heart and to profess openly. I most certainly do not remember when the priest put the "blessed salt" in my mouth, which was said to be an emblem of Christian wisdom and of preservation from the corruption of sin. After this ceremony had taken place at the entrance of the church, where the baptismal font is located, while held in the arms of my godmother I was led by the stole of the priest into the church, thus signifying that I was admitted as a member. Such is the papal ceremony of baptism. It is described thus by a Jesuit:

> "The other ceremonies of baptism are also very ancient, and have all a deep meaning. 1. The person to be baptized remains at first without the church, because only baptism gives him entrance into it. 2. The priest breathes three times in his face, to signify the new and spiritual life he receives by the grace of the Holy Ghost (Genesis 2: 7, and John 20:22). 3. The sign of the cross made upon his forehead and upon his breast denotes that he is becoming the property of his crucified Redeemer, whose doctrine he is to carry in his heart, and to profess openly. 4. The blessed salt, which is put into his mouth, is an emblem of Christian wisdom, and of preservation from the corruption of sin. 5. By the exorcisms, which are repeated several times, the power of the devil, 'who has the empire of death' (Hebrews 2: 14), is broken in the name of the Blessed Trinity. 6. The laying of the priest's hand upon the person to be baptized signifies the protection of God; and the stole laid upon him, and his being led by it into the church, is a sign of the ecclesiastical power, in virtue of which the priest admits him into the church. 7. The touching of the child's ears and nostrils with spittle, in imitation of our Saviour (Mark 7: 33), signifies that, by the grace of this sacrament, his spiritual senses are opened to the doctrine of Christ. 8. After having renounced the devil and all his works, and all his pomps, he is anointed with holy oil on the breast and between the shoulders, because, as a champion of Christ, be has now manfully to fight against the devil and the world. 9. After the baptism, the crown of the head is anointed with chrism, to intimate that he Is now a Christian—i.e., an anointed of God, etc."[8]

The Roman Catholic Church teaches that baptism serves two purposes: (1) the washing away of the original sin, and (2) the admitting of the child as a member into the church. "Original sin...is universal. Every child is, therefore, defiled at its birth with the taint of Adam's

---

[8] Joseph Deharbe, S. J., *A Complete Catechism of the Catholic Religion*, 6th American ed. (New York: Schwartz, Kirwin & Fauss, 1924) 255.

disobedience....Hence baptism, which washes away original sin, is as essential for the infant as for the full grown man, in order to attain the kingdom of heaven."[9]

This doctrine of infant baptism has given rise to the invention of the *limbus infantium* (the limbo of infants). The papal teaching on this subject is not only cruel, but it misrepresents God's great love toward the helpless. If there is anything in which Satan delights, it is a doctrine that pictures the Lord as unsympathetic and inexorable in His dealings with the human family.

The *limbus infantium* is something every Roman Catholic mother fears who has an unbaptized infant. Many wonder why the conscientious Roman Catholic mother will rush her newborn babe to the church to be baptized by the priest. The following excerpt will show that the papacy, in the fifth session of the Council of Trent, not only reaffirmed the doctrine of infant baptism, but anathematizes those who deny or treat this rite lightly:

"Whoever shall affirm that children are not to be reckoned among the faithful by the reception of baptism, because they do not actually believe; and therefore that they are to be rebaptized when they come to years of discretion; or that, since they cannot personally believe, it is better to omit their baptism, than that they should be baptized only in the faith of the church: let him be accursed."

"Whosoever shall affirm, that newborn infants, even though sprung from baptized parents, ought not to be baptized, etc., let him be accursed.

"Whosoever shall deny that the guilt of original sin is remitted by the grace of our Lord Jesus Christ, bestowed in baptism, etc. If any one thinks differently, let him be accursed."[10]

---

9 Gibbons, 271.
10 John Dowling, *The History of Romanism*, 7th ed. (New York: Edward Walker, 1845) 510, 499.

When one is conversant with the belief that were a child to die before baptism, it would be consigned to the "limbo of infants" where it would never see the light of God, and throughout eternity would be barred from heaven and from the association of the saved, he can readily understand why hasty steps are taken to have a newborn child baptized.

"It is proper here to state briefly what the [Roman Catholic] Church actually teaches regarding the future state of unbaptized infants. Though the church, in obedience to God's word, declares that unbaptized infants are excluded from the kingdom of heaven, it should not hence be concluded that they are consigned to the place of the reprobate. None are condemned to the torments of the damned but such as merit divine vengeance by their personal sins.

"All that the church holds on this point is that unregenerate children are deprived of the beatific vision, or the possession of God, which constitutes the essential happiness of the blessed.

"Now, between the supreme bliss of heaven and the torments of the reprobate, there is a very wide margin.

"All admit that the condition of unbaptized infants is better than non-existence. There are some Catholic writers of distinction who even assert that unbaptized infants enjoy a certain degree of natural beatitude—that is, a happiness which is based on the natural knowledge and love of God.

"From what has been said you may well judge how reprehensible is the conduct of Catholic parents who neglect to have their children baptized at the earliest possible moment, thereby risking their own souls, as well as the souls of their innocent offspring."[11]

One can imagine that after the inculcation of such teaching by a supposedly inerrant church, the bereaved mother of an unbaptized infant greatly suffers mentally when she thinks that she will not only be deprived of the

---
[11] Gibbons, 273.

companionship of her child in the hereafter, but also that her little one will never experience the blissful enjoyment of heaven. A Roman Catholic work gives an interesting history of the inception of the doctrine of the limbo of infants, and of the discussion that ensued among the outstanding papal theologians:

"*Limbus Infantium* — It is an article of faith that those who die without baptism, and in whose case the want of baptism has not been supplied in some other way, cannot enter heaven. This is plainly stated, e.g., by the Council of Florence in the Decree of Union. But there was a natural repugnance to the belief that those who had committed no sin should be tortured in hell, and this difficulty led theologians to adopt various theories as by way of escape.

"1. Some few theologians thought that God might be pleased to supply the want of baptism in infants by other means. Thus St. Bernard (*De Baptismo,* c.i.n.4,c.ii.n.1) thought that possibly such infants might be saved by the faith of their parents. A similar opinion is attributed to Gerson, Cardinal Cajetan and others — viz. that the lack of baptism might be supplied by the wish for the sacrament on the part of their parents or others; Cajetan requiring in addition the use of some external sign with the invocation of the Trinity. (See Billuart, *De Baptism.* diss. iii. a. 1.)

"Another theologian, Albertus a Balsano (*Compend. Theol.* vol. ii, sec. 325, quoted by Jungmann, *De Noviss.*), believed that God might commission angels to confer baptism on infants who might otherwise perish without it.

"2. The theologians of the Augustinian order (e.g. Cardinal Noris and Berti) held an opinion at the opposite pole — viz. that the infants in question were punished both by exclusion from heaven and by positive pain, though much less pain than is inflicted on those who die in actual mortal sin. This undoubtedly is the opinion of St. Augustine (*Serm.* 294, where he teaches that unbaptized infants were consigned to eternal fire), though their damnation will be 'the lightest of all' (*De Peccat. Meritis et Remiss.* i. 20).

"3. The great majority of theoloigians—the Master of the Sentences, St. Buonaventure, St. Thomas, Scotus, etc.,—teach that infants dying in original sin suffer no 'pain of sense,' but are simply excluded from heaven. This opinion is no modern invention, for it is found in St. Gregory Nazianzen (*Or. in Saws. Baptism.* 23). But do they grieve because they are shut out of heaven? Bellarmin (*De Amiss. Gratiae, vi. 6,* apud Jungmann) answers Yes. St. Thomas answers that they do not, because pain of punishment is proportioned to personal guilt, which does not exist here. He says they do not grieve because they cannot see God, any more than a bird is grieved because it cannot be emperor or king: 'nay, they rejoice, because they share in God's goodness and in many natural perfections.' The opinion of St. Thomas is the common one in the church. It is believed that unbaptized infants in Limbo know and love God by the use of their natural powers, and have full natural happiness."[12]

After reading this statement of the views of "the fathers" of the Roman Catholic Church on the destiny of unbaptized infants, and after observing the diversified opinions given on this subject, one may well ask: Which theory is correct? Such teachings cannot stand the test of the word of God.

Ought an infant to be baptized at birth? One searches the Book of God in vain for one text teaching infant baptism. The apostle Peter gives us some very concrete instructions in regard to baptism, and mentions the steps which a person must take in order to receive this sacred rite: "Then Peter said unto them, Repent, and be baptized every one of you in the name of Jesus Christ for the remission of sins, and ye shall receive the gift of the Holy Ghost." [Acts 2:38]

An infant cannot repent of sin nor comprehend the doctrine of original sin, because it is wholly incapable of discerning between good and evil. Furthermore, Jesus is

---

[12] Wm. E. Addis and Thom. Arnold, "Limbo," *A Catholic Dictionary*, 2d ed. (London: Kegan Paul, Trench & Company, 1884) 518, 519.

Infant Baptism

our example and authority in all things, especially in matters of doctrine. When He was baptized, He was old enough to understand what He was doing. "Then cometh Jesus from Galilee to Jordan unto John, to be baptized of him. But John forbad Him, saying, I have need to be baptized of Thee, and comest Thou to me? And Jesus answering said unto him, Suffer it to be so now: for thus it becometh us to fulfill all righteousness. Then he suffered Him." [Matt. 3:13-15]

Christ's command is that instruction be given to the new believer before he receives baptism, thus enabling him to be fully baptized into the name and character of the Father, the Son, and the Holy Spirit. "Go ye therefore, and teach all nations, baptizing them in the name of the Father, and of the Son, and of the Holy Ghost: teaching them to observe all things whatsoever I have commanded you." [Matt. 28:19, 20] Christ emphasizes not only the instruction but also the conformity to all that He commanded.

We have on record the experience of the Ethiopian eunuch Acts [8:35–38], whom Philip instructed in the word of God prior to his baptism, thus showing the necessity of being conversant with the plan of salvation before receiving the sacred rite.

Another important point for consideration is the mode of baptism. While God's word teaches that there is only one baptism [Eph. 4:5], the Roman Catholic Church offers a choice of three:

> "Baptism may be validly administered in either of three ways, viz: by *immersion*, or by plunging the candidate into the water; by *infusion*, or by pouring the water; and by *aspersion*, or sprinkling....The church exercises her discretion in adopting the most convenient mode, according to the circumstances of time and place.
>
> "For several centuries after the establishment of Christianity baptism was *usually* conferred by immersion; but since the twelfth century the practice of baptizing by

infusion has prevailed in the [Roman] Catholic Church, as this manner is attended with less inconvenience than baptism by immersion."[13]

"The most ancient form usually employed was unquestionably immersion. This is not only evident from the writings of the Fathers and the early rituals of both the Latin and Oriental Churches, but it can also be gathered from the Epistles of St. Paul, who speaks of baptism as a bath (Ephesians 5: 26; Romans 6: 4; Titus 3: 5). In the Latin Church, immersion seems to have prevailed until the twelfth century. After that time it is found in some places even as late as the sixteenth century. Infusion and aspersion, however, were growing common in the thirteenth century and gradually prevailed in the Western Church. The Oriental Churches have retained immersion."[14]

"[Roman] Catholics admit that immersion brings out more fully the meaning of the sacrament (Romans 6: 3, 4; Colossians 2: 12; Titus 3: 5; Ephesians 5: 27), and that for twelve centuries it was the common practice....The [Greek] Orthodox always baptize by immersion, and erroneously think it so necessary that they doubt the validity of any other kind of baptism. They have gone so far as to rebaptize all Latins who joined their church (1756, Synod of Constantinople, 111, Q. 66, art. 7)."[15]

"There is no express mention of the baptizing of infants in the New Testament."[16]

In studying the mode which Jesus followed in baptism, do we find any record that He had a linen cloth placed on His head, or had a lighted candle put in His hand by John? No, the word of God says nothing in behalf of all these liturgical objects. The baptismal font and the priest were lacking. Neither was there any stole used by John to lead Christ into the church. We do not find recorded the names

---

13   Gibbons, 277.
14   "Baptism," *The Catholic Encyclopedia*, v2, 261, 262.
15   Bertrand L. Conway, *The Question Box*, new ed. (New York: The Paulist Press, 1920) 240.
16   Ibid., 243.

Infant Baptism

of any godmother or godfather to Christ. On the contrary, instead of following all this ritual and ceremony, He wended His way to the river Jordan, and when John administered the rite of baptism, they both went down into the water and Christ was immersed. [Matt. 3:13–17; Mark 1:9, 10] In the early Christian church there was no baptismal font wherein was a small quantity of water to be used in administering the rite of baptism. The real mode of baptism calls for much water. "And John also was baptizing in Ænon near to Salim, because there was *much water* there: and they came, and were baptized." [John 3:23]

Paul, the apostle, also gives further light on baptism and presents it as a memorial of the burial and resurrection of the Son of God. "What shall we say then? Shall we continue in sin, that grace may abound? God forbid. How shall we, that are dead to sin, live any longer therein? Know ye not, that so many of us as were baptized into Jesus Christ were baptized into His death? Therefore we are buried with Him by baptism into death: that like as Christ was raised up from the dead by the glory of the Father, even so we also should walk in newness of life. For if we have been planted together in the likeness of His death, we shall be also in the likeness of His resurrection." [Rom. 6:1–5]

As the new believer goes down into the watery grave, he is buried with his Lord in baptism; and as he comes forth, he testifies that he believes in the death, the burial, and the resurrection of the Son of God. The performance of this rite is an acknowledgment on the part of the baptized one that he has died to the world and to sin, and that his past life is buried in the death of his Saviour. just as Christ came forth from the grave victorious, so the recipient of this ordinance comes forth from the waters of baptism a victor over the enemy; and henceforth he is to walk in perfect accord with the law of God.

It is the Roman Catholic Church that has extended to men the cup from which baptism by sprinkling and pouring have issued. The Inspired Record states that "the inhabitants of the earth have been made drunk with the wine of her fornication." This prophecy has been fulfilled literally by those Protestant churches which have continued to sip the papal beverage of infant baptism and the practice of sprinkling and pouring.

If the Holy Bible is the only guide for Protestants to follow, then why do they accept the teaching of tradition on certain points of faith? The Protestant pledge gives no place for adherence to man-made doctrines. Listen to these words by the Protestant historian, John Dowling:

> "'The Bible, I say, the Bible only, is the religion of Protestants!' Nor is it of any account in the estimation of the genuine Protestant, how early a doctrine originated, if it is not found in the Bible....Hence if a doctrine be propounded for his acceptance, he asks, is it to be found in the Inspired Word? was it taught by the Lord Jesus Christ, and His apostles? If they knew nothing of it, no matter to him, whether it be discovered in the musty folio of some ancient visionary of the third or fourth century, or whether it springs from the fertile brain of some modern visionary of the nineteenth, if it is not found in the Sacred Scriptures, it presents no valid claim to be received as an article of his religious creed,...And he who receives a single doctrine upon the mere authority of tradition, let him be called by what name he will, by so doing, steps down from the Protestant rock, passes over the line which separates Protestantism from popery, and can give no valid reason why he should not receive all the earlier doctrines and ceremonies of Romanism, upon the same authority."[17]

When we stand before God in the judgment, how wonderful to be able to take our stand on His Written Word and look into the face of Him and say, "Lord, I have carried out Thy commands, I have followed closely what I

---
[17] Dowling, 67, 68.

have read concerning the manner in which Christ was baptized, and have received that sacred rite according as His example indicated." The words of Christ's approbation would mean more to one than all the vain glory that attends the ritualistic service of the apostate church.

The Lord does not hold man accountable on any point of doctrine until enlightenment comes; but He does expect His commands to be definitely carried out when man becomes conversant with them. "To him that knoweth to do good, and doeth it not, to him it is sin." [James 4:17] When light shines from God's word into a person's heart, He demands obedience from him. "And the times of this ignorance God winked at; but now commandeth all men every where to repent." [Acts 17:30] There is only one course left for those who have been sprinkled, and that is to follow Christ's example and be immersed. "For as many of you as have been baptized into Christ have put on Christ." [Gal. 3:27]

Also see Appendix p. 193.

Many Protestant churches ape the Roman sect in the practice of infant baptism by sprinkling. In some cases the Protestant minister even uses the same baptismal words as does the Roman priest. This photo shows an Episcopalian minister in a christening service. The fact that there is just one sponsor, a man, shows that the baby is a boy. (Photo by Acme.)

CHAPTER IV

Auricular Confession

THE THIRD sip from the cup of Babylon is known as "Auricular Confession." This doctrine was reaffirmed by the Council of Trent, and the Tridentine curses are hurled against those who reject it as a divine institution. So we read:

"Whoever shall deny that sacramental confession was instituted by divine command, or that it is necessary to salvation; or shall affirm that the practice of secretly confessing to the priest alone, as it has been ever observed from the beginning by the [Roman] Catholic Church, and is still observed, is foreign to the institution and command of Christ, and is a human invention: let him be accursed.

"Whoever shall affirm, that in order to obtain forgiveness of sins in the sacrament of penance, it is not by divine command necessary to confess all and every mortal sin which occurs to the memory after due and diligent premeditation — including secret offences, etc.: let him be accursed.

"Whoever shall affirm that the confession of every sin, according to the custom of the [Roman] Church, is impossible, and merely a human tradition, which the pious should reject; or that all Christians, of both sexes, are not bound to observe the same once a year, according to the constitution of the great Council of Lateran; and therefore, that the faithful in Christ are to be persuaded not to confess in Lent: let him be accursed.

"Whoever shall affirm that the priest's sacramental absolution is not a judicial act, but only a ministry, to pronounce and declare that the sins of the party confessing are forgiven, so that he believes himself to be absolved, even though the priest should not absolve seriously, but in jest; or shall affirm that the confession of the penitent is not necessary in order to obtain absolution from the priest: let him be accursed."[18]

The third commandment of the Roman Catholic Church requires confession, and failure to obey this ecclesiastical ordinance theoretically excludes the disobedient from membership and church burial.

"The third commandment of the [Roman Catholic] Church obliges us to go to confession once a year. This law was enacted at the Fourth Council of Lateran in the year of 1215. The penalty attached to the violation of this law is, that the sinner may be interdicted from entering the church while living, and be deprived of Christian burial when dead.

"Our Lord Himself made it an obligation for sinners to confess their sins, when He instituted the sacrament of penance. Hence the law of the church merely reminds sinners of their duty to confess their sins, and fixes the time within which this duty must be performed. A bad confession does not satisfy the law.

"By declaring that, under pain of mortal sin, we must confess our sins at least once a year, the church implies that we should go to confession frequently during the year; and she exhorts her devoted children to confess their sins even once a week.

"The church leaves us free to choose any confessor who is authorized by the bishop to hear confessions.

"This law of the church is binding on all who have attained the use of reason. Therefore as soon as children can distinguish between right and wrong, so as to be capable of mortal sin, they ought to be prepared for their first confession."[19]

If auricular confession was ordained by Christ, the Founder of the Christian church, why should 1,200 years be allowed to pass before imposing the obligation

---

18   Dowling, 515.
19   Butler, 203.

Auricular Confession

requiring members to go to confession and receive communion at least once a year? Did the Lord change the plan of salvation after 12 centuries had passed by, permitting the institution of the auricular confession, and anathematizing all who should reject it? Our Lord never changes, and He has not altered His plan of salvation. "I am the Lord, I change not." [Mal. 3:6] "Jesus Christ the same yesterday, and today, and for ever." [Heb. 13:8] "My covenant will I not break, nor alter the thing that is gone out of My lips." [Ps. 89:34]

The introduction of the doctrine of auricular confession gave to the priesthood great power. Note this statement by a papal prelate:

"As far as heaven is above earth, as eternity is above time, and the soul is above the body, so far are the prerogatives vested in God's ministers higher than those of any earthly potentate. An earthly prince can cast into prison or release therefrom. But his power is over the body. He cannot penetrate into the sanctuary of the soul; whereas the minister of God can release the soul from the prison of sin, and restore it to the liberty of a child of God. To sum up in a few brief sentences the titles of a [Roman] Catholic priest: He is a *king*, reigning not over unwilling subjects, but over the hearts and affections of his people....He is a *shepherd*, because he leads his flock into the delicious pastures of the sacraments....He is a *father*, because he breaks the bread of life to his spiritual children....He is a *judge*, whose office it is to pass sentence of pardon on self-accusing criminals. He is a *physician*, because he heals their souls from the loathsome distempers of sin."[20]

Another writer observes:

"Seek where you will, through heaven and earth, and you will find but one created being who can forgive the sinner, who can free him from the chains of hell, that extraordinary being is the priest, the [Roman] Catholic priest. 'Who can forgive sins except God?' was the question which the

---
[20] Gibbons, 390, 391.

The Wine of Roman Babylon

Pharisees sneeringly asked. 'Who can forgive sins?' is the question which the Pharisees of the present day also ask, and I answer there is a man on earth that can forgive sins, and that man is the [Roman] Catholic priest. Yes, beloved brethren, the priest not only declares that the sinner is forgiven, but he *really forgives him*. The priest raises his hand, he pronounces the word of absolution, and in an instant, quick as a flash of light the chains of hell are burst asunder, and the sinner becomes a child of God. So great is the power of the priest that the judgments of heaven itself are subject to his decision."[21]

What happened to all those souls who had not confessed their sins to a priest for forgiveness during the first 1,200 years of the Christian era? How were the sins of those who lived during the 4,000 years before Christ expiated without the confessional, penance, and satisfaction?

Nowhere in the word of God are we furnished an instance where the Lord has abdicated in favor of a human being. But the papacy teaches that its priests can absolve from sin those who confess to them.

"Q. Does St. Ambrose say that priests have the power to forgive sins? A. St. Ambrose says: 'It seems impossible for sins to be forgiven by penitence, but Christ granted this to His apostles, which has been from the apostles transmitted to the ministry of the priests.'"[22]

"The [Roman] Church teaches that our Lord conferred on the apostles a true priesthood, when He gave them power to offer the sacrifice of the mass and the power to forgive sins. By the possession of these two powers the apostles were constituted true priests, or mediators between God and man."[23]

---

[21] Muller, 78, 79.
[22] Roderick MacEachen, *Complete Catechism of Christian Doctrine*, rev. ed. (Wheeling: Catholic Book Co., 1911) 120, 121.
[23] Butler, 277.

Auricular Confession

The Lord has. never given to man the power to absolve from sin. "Who can forgive sins, but God alone?" [Luke 5:21] The apostle Peter evidently knew nothing about auricular confession, absolution, penance, or satisfaction, when he dealt with the sin of Simon the sorcerer. Peter told Simon to pray to God for the forgiveness of sin. [Acts 8:22]

The priest claims the power to sit in judgment on the sins of men, declaring himself to be another Christ. Here is a striking declaration on this point:

> "Not content with humbly submitting Himself [Christ] to the will of the priest, God has given him the right to sit in judgment on the sins of men and release them from the debt they owe to His offended majesty.
>
> "'Go, show yourselves to the priest,' He said, 'he is My representative on earth, holding in his hands the power of God. No matter what your sins may be, no matter how numerous or repeated times without number, if only he forgives you, so shall I. His authority, his right to forgive is absolute, for I have said to him: "Whatsoever you shall bind upon earth, shall be bound also in heaven; and whatsoever you shall loose upon earth, shall be loosed also in heaven."'
>
> "Confident in that promise, for 'God is faithful and cannot deceive,' the poor sinner kneels at his confessor's feet. He knows he is not speaking to an ordinary man but to 'another Christ,' and humbly but trustfully pours into his ear the secrets of his soul.... What he [the sinner] has said no one will ever know; sorrow fills his heart, he hears the words: 'I absolve thee from thy sins in the name of the Father, Son, and Holy Ghost,' and the hideous load of sin drops from his soul for ever."[24]

The confessing of sin is a very important and solemn matter, and ought not to be done lightly. The word of God has much to say about the acknowledging and forsaking of sins, but never does it state that we are to go to a man, kneel at his feet, and pour into his ear all the evil thoughts,

---
24 Doyle, 14, 15.

words, and acts of our lives. In the auricular confession all the sins that are not voluntarily confessed are extracted by "prudent questions" asked by the priest. We are told:

"The [Roman] Church teaches that we are bound to confess each and every mortal sin that we have committed, even sins of thought and desire, as well as the circumstances that change the species of the sin. Hence, we are strictly bound to confess each mortal sin, so that each grievous sin may be directly forgiven by the absolution of the priest. It is not enough to tell the number of our sins, we must also name the species of the sin, that is, we must state the special law or virtue that was violated by it. If we cannot tell the exact number of our sins, we should tell the number as nearly as possible."[25]

Every Roman Catholic, old and young, is taught that he must adhere to the instruction which is given in the catechism regarding the confession of sins. For example:

"Q. How do you begin your confession? A. Having... arrived at the confessional, I kneel down, make the sign of the cross, and ask the priest's blessing by saying: 'Bless me, Father, for I have sinned.' After receiving his blessing, I say the first part of the *confiteor*."[26]

The *confiteor* ("I confess") is described in the following extract:

"I confess to Almighty God, to the blessed Mary ever virgin, to blessed Michael the archangel, to blessed John the Baptist, to the holy apostles Peter and Paul, and to all the saints, that I have sinned exceedingly in thought, word and deed; through my fault, through my fault, through my most grievous fault."[27]

After repeating this prayer of confession to God, to Mary, and to the various saints, the suppliant continues by unfolding to his priestly confessor the sins that he has committed, and concludes thus:

---

25   Butler, 267.
26   Deharbe, 290, 291.
27   MacEachen, 12.

Auricular Confession

"I am heartily sorry, purpose amendment for the future, and most humbly ask pardon of God, and penance and absolution of you, my ghostly father."[28]

It is said that one of the essential parts of the confession is the repeating of the first part of the *confiteor*, as follows:

"Therefore, I beseech the blessed Mary ever virgin, blessed Michael the archangel, blessed John the Baptist, the holy apostles Peter and Paul, and all the saints, to pray to the Lord our God for me. May the Almighty God have mercy on me, forgive me my sins, and bring me to life everlasting. Amen. May the almighty and merciful Lord grant me pardon, absolution and remission of all my sins. Amen."[29]

The Holy Bible gives many examples of what constitutes confession, true repentance, and forgiveness. We have the experience of the publican who went to the temple to seek God for pardon. "And the publican, standing afar off, would not lift up so much as his eyes unto heaven, but smote upon his breast, saying, God be merciful to me a sinner. I tell you, this man went down to his house justified." [Luke 18: 13, 14] This man did not go to a confessional box, kneel before a priest, invoke his blessing and pardon, and he did not repeat the confiteor. He appealed — directly — to God for forgiveness, and forthwith it was granted, without requiring any penance to be performed as satisfaction for his sins.

God, knowing the publican's heart and accepting his repentance, granted him pardon. Thus the Holy Scriptures teach that God alone can forgive sin, and that He demands no satisfaction. What He requires is not penance but repentance, which is the turning away from sin. [Prov. 28:13; Ezek. 33: 14, 15] The papal doctrine of the auricular confession and the human priesthood takes away from Christ His prerogative as the One who can forgive sins. "Who is a God like unto Thee, that pardoneth iniquity, and passeth

---

[28] Deharbe, 291.
[29] MacEachen, 12.

by the transgression of the remnant of His heritage? He retaineth not His anger forever, because He delighteth in mercy. He will turn again, He will have compassion upon us; He will subdue our iniquities; and Thou wilt cast all their sins into the depths of the sea." [Mic. 7: 18, 19]

There is no uncertainty concerning the absolution which the Lord grants to the one who will confess his sin and by faith lay hold of His promise of pardon. "If we confess our sins, He is faithful and just to forgive us our sins, and to cleanse us from all unrighteousness." [1 John 1:9] How can anyone kneel before a human priest, to pour into his ears the very secrets of his heart, and put aside the blessed invitation given by Jesus, our great High Priest, who will exchange our scarlet robe of sin for the snow-white garment of righteousness, and the crimson-like rags of iniquity for the wool-like covering of Christ's own life! [Isa. 1:18]

Also see Appendix p. 197.

CHAPTER V

Penance

THE FOURTH sip from Babylon's cup we shall name "Penance." The Council of Trent, in its fourteenth session, issued its famous decree on penance as a sacrament:

"Whoever shall affirm that penance, as used in the [Roman] Catholic Church is not truly and properly a sacrament, instituted by Christ our Lord, for the benefit of the faithful, to reconcile them to God, as often as they shall fall into sin after baptism: let him be accursed.

"Whoever, confounding the sacraments, shall affirm that baptism itself is a penance, as if those two sacraments were not distinct, and penance were not rightly called a 'second plank after shipwreck': let him be accursed....

"Whoever shall deny, that in order to the full and perfect forgiveness of sins, three acts are required of the penitent, constituting as it were the matter of the sacrament of penance, namely, contrition, confession, and satisfaction, which are called the three parts of penance; or shall affirm that there are only two parts of penance, namely, terrors wherewith the conscience is smitten by the sense of sin, and faith, produced by the gospel, or by absolution, whereby the person believes that his sins are forgiven him through Christ: let him be accursed."[30]

An examination of this doctrine reveals that it contains many ingredients, "namely, contrition, confession, and satisfaction. The definition in the Roman Catholic Catechism is as follows:

---
[30] Dowling, 514, 515.

"Q. What do we mean by penance? A. By a penance we mean the prayers of good works imposed by the priest in confession. It is intended as satisfaction for our sins....Q. What punishment for sin is taken away by the sacrament of penance? A. The eternal punishment for sin is taken away in the sacrament of penance. Q. What is meant by the temporal punishment of sin? A. The temporal punishment of sin is that punishment which is due after the guilt of the sin is forgiven."[31]

"In this sacrament sins are forgiven by the priest's absolution, joined with contrition, confession and satisfaction on the part of the penitent....It also remits the eternal, and at least a part of the temporal, punishment due to our past sins."[32]

The sacraments of penance and auricular confession are very closely connected. It is in the confessional that penance is imposed by the priest. By performing the good works, the penal suffering is offered as satisfaction for sin to God by the penitent, which is truly an admission by the priest that they have not full faith in their absolution.

What a picture to hang before a poor soul who is weighted down with the burden of sin! What is left after confession but to resort to his own Works to redeem himself from sin? The round of meritorious works keeps the soul bound to its sins, wearies the body, and banishes peace from the mind. What a different experience comes with the knowledge of sins forgiven by the Redeemer of the world!

The doctrine of penance is diametrically opposed to what the Holy Scriptures teach on justification by faith. It does away with a loving and merciful Saviour, and causes the individual to lose confidence in the assurance of full salvation through Him. The papal church has left nothing undone to elevate man and his own works, thereby

---

[31] MacEachen, 126.
[32] Butler, 257.

robbing God of His rightful place in the hearts of men. How tragic to see souls laboring under such false delusions and trying to offer meaningless works as a satisfaction to an all-loving God! God asks us: "Can the Ethiopian change his skin, or the leopard his spots? Then may ye also do good, that are accustomed to do evil." [Jer. 13:23] "Without Me ye can do nothing." [John 15:5]

God never intended that His children should be kept in doubt as to their eternal salvation. The promise of God's complete forgiveness is as certain as His word, so that not only mortal but venial sins will be pardoned, as the word "all" in the following text indicates: "If we confess our sins, He is faithful and just to forgive us our sins, and to cleanse us from all unrighteousness." [1 John 1:9] "Come now, and let us reason together, saith the Lord: though your sins be as scarlet, they shall be as white as snow; though they be red like crimson, they shall be as wool." [Isa. 1:18]

It is the rending of the heart and not outward works for which God calls. "Therefore also now, saith the Lord, turn ye even to Me with all your heart, and with fasting, and with weeping, and with mourning: and rend your heart, and not your garments, and turn unto the Lord your God: for He is gracious and merciful, slow to anger, and of great kindness, and repenteth Him of the evil." [Joel 2:12, 13] From the days of Cain, who was the first to introduce his own works as a substitute for Christ's pardoning power, until now the enemy of all righteousness has left nothing undone to blind man to his utter dependence upon God alone for salvation.

John the Baptist did not impose penance, but he taught repentance to those who came to him for baptism. "Bring forth therefore fruits meet for repentance."[33] When Christ pardoned the adulterous woman, penance was not meted

---

[33] Matthew 3:8. The revised *Roman Catholic New Testament* gives Matthew 3:8 thus: "Bring forth therefore fruit befitting repentance." The Douay Version (Roman Catholic) says "penance" instead of "repentance."

by Him to the penitent, but He did require repentance, as His words of counsel attest: "Go, and sin no more." [John 8:11]

In replying to the question, "What shall we do?" asked by hearts convicted of sin, the apostle Peter said nothing about the sacrament of penance, as his inspired reply discloses: "Now when they heard this, they were pricked in their heart, and said unto Peter and to the rest of the apostles, Men and brethren, what shall we do? Then Peter said unto them, Repent."[34]

The doctrine of repentance was the great burden of Peter's teaching. "Repent ye therefore, and be converted, that your sins may be blotted out, when the times of refreshing shall come from the presence of the Lord."[35] There is a vast difference between doing penance and repenting of sins. It is easier for the carnal mind to repeat the litany or rosary than to surrender the will to God and relinquish cherished sins. By one's own works of penance he virtually denies the redemption accomplished by Christ on the cross. Justification, and not satisfaction, is the teaching of the Holy Bible. What can the good works of a poor mortal accomplish in satisfying the claims of the broken law of a holy and merciful, but just God?

In the papal "tribunal of penance" the priestly scale measures out to the penitent an amount of good works to be done not only for the purpose of satisfying the justice of God, but also for expiating the sins that he has committed. Here is the way Roman Catholics are taught to regard it:

"Penance is a sacrament of the new law instituted by Christ in which forgiveness of sins committed after baptism

---

[34] Acts 2:37, 38. The revised *Roman Catholic New Testament* gives Peter's reply thus: "Repent and be baptized every one of you in the name of Jesus Christ for the forgiveness of your sins." The Douay Version says: "Do penance" instead of "Repent."

[35] Acts 3:19. "Repent therefore and be converted, that your sins may be blotted out," says the revised *Roman Catholic New Testament*.

is granted through the priest's absolution to those who with true sorrow confess their sins and promise to satisfy for the same. It is called a 'sacrament' not simply a function or ceremony, because it is an outward sign instituted by Christ to impart grace to the soul. As an outward sign it comprises the actions of the penitent in presenting himself to the priest and accusing himself of his sins, and the actions of the priest in pronouncing absolution and imposing satisfaction. The whole procedure is usually called, from one of its parts, 'confession'; and it is said to take place in the 'tribunal of penance,' because it is a judicial process in which the penitent is at once the accuser, the person accused, and the witness, while the priest pronounces judgment and sentence. The grace conferred is deliverance from the guilt of sin and, in the case of mortal sin, from Its eternal punishment; hence also reconciliation with God, justification. Finally, the confession is made not in the secrecy of the penitent's heart nor to a layman's friend and advocate, nor to a representative of human authority, but to a duly ordained priest with requisite jurisdiction and with the 'power of the keys,' i.e., the power to forgive sins, which Christ granted to His church."[36]

In the Roman Catholic Church the inflexible requirements imposed in the sacrament of penance cannot be averted, however contrite the heart of the sinner may be in the confessional. Jesus, who "died for our sins," and who says to the sinner, "I, even I, am He that blotteth out thy transgressions for Mine own sake, and, will not remember thy sins," [1 Cor. 15:3; Isa. 43:25] is never held up by the priest as man's perfect atonement.

The Inspired Word teaches that it is either grace absolutely, or works absolutely: "And if by grace, then is it no more of works: otherwise grace is no more grace. But if it be of works, then is it no more grace: otherwise work is no more work." [Rom. 11:6] Not until confession of sin and the entire renunciation of everything that is offensive to

---
[36] "Penance," *The Catholic Encyclopedia*, v2, 618, 619.

God is made, will the imputed righteousness of Christ be credited, without works, to the account of the sinner. "Even as David also describeth the blessedness of the man, unto whom God imputeth righteousness without works, saying, Blessed are they whose iniquities are forgiven, and whose sins are covered." [Rom. 4:6, 7]

The Roman Catholic Church teaches that it is not only necessary to receive absolution in the confessional, but that through the sacrament of penance the imposing of the performance of good works is essential, thus advocating salvation through a combination of grace and works.

It is our acceptance of Christ by faith as our propitiation that brings about the remission of our sins. For it is He "whom God hath set forth to be a propitiation through faith in His blood, to declare His righteousness for the remission of sins that are past, through the forbearance of God." [Rom. 3:25] There is no more condemnation, fear is all gone, and the peace of heaven abides in the heart of those who accept God's plan. "There is therefore now no condemnation to them which are in Christ Jesus, who walk not after the flesh, but after the Spirit." [Rom. 8:1]

Also see Appendix p. 199.

CHAPTER VI

The Mass

THE FIFTH sip from the cup of Babylon is here named "The Mass," which plays an important part in the life of every true Roman Catholic. This institution is used more effectively than any other to bind the communicants to that church. In their own language:

"The holy eucharist is the greatest and most wonderful of the seven sacraments. It is the divine center of all [Roman] Catholic worship. It is the greatest of the mysteries of our faith, a compendium of all the other mysteries.... It further differs from the other sacraments and excels them."[37]

The mass, from beginning to end, is so dramatic that it impresses forcibly those who are present, whether learned or unlearned. As those in the audience watch the expressive actions and gestures of the officiating priest, from the moment he bows at the foot of the altar until he leaves, they are so captivated with such sacerdotal performances that they do not think to question their authenticity. The fact that this service is in Latin gives it an air of mystery, elegance, and scholarship, which the common intellect is incapable of comprehending or explaining. There is nothing left undone to appeal to the senses and dazzle the eye. The lights, that illuminate the altar and cause the handiwork of man to sparkle, the rich vestments, and the smoke of the incense are all designed to charm and yet subdue the spectator.

---
[37] Butler, 241.

The Wine of Roman Babylon

To explain more fully the mystery of the mass and the liturgical objects and the part each one plays in the great drama, I give this list:

"The altar represents Mount Calvary on which our Lord died. The crucifix represents our Lord hanging on the cross. The altar-cloths represent the linen in which the dead body of our Saviour was wrapped. The lighted candles represent our Lord as the light of the world; and are also an emblem of Christian faith, hope and charity. The sanctuary lamp represents the star of Bethlehem pointing out the humble abode of the King of kings. The tabernacle represents the cave of Bethlehem, the abode of the divine Saviour. The tabernacle veil reminds us of the hidden presence of our Lord in the blessed sacrament. The chalice represents the cup in which our Lord consecrated at the Last Supper. The corporal, a square piece of linen, commemorates the winding-sheet in which our Saviour was buried. The missal is the book in which the prayers and ceremonies of the mass are contained. The bell, rung at certain times during mass, gives notice of the most solemn parts of the sacrifice. Incense is a symbol of prayer rising to heaven. The vestments of the priest remind us of the sufferings of our Saviour whom the priest represents. The amice represents Christ blindfolded and buffeted. The alb represents the white garment which Herod put on our Lord. The cincture represents the cord with which our Lord was bound. The maniple is a symbol of sorrow, and recalls the tears and disfigured countenance of our Lord. The stole is the sign of priestly power, and recalls the cord with which our Lord was bound during the passion. The chasuble represents Jesus Christ clothed by Pilate in a purple garment. White vestments symbolize purity. Red vestments symbolize fortitude. Purple vestments symbolize penance. Green vestments symbolize hope. Black vestments symbolize sorrow."[38]

One searches the Holy Scriptures in vain to find mention of the liturgy of the mass. The objects which the Roman Catholic Church deems necessary in the performance of

---

38   Ibid., 327, 328.

The Mass

the mass are foreign to the word of God, for Christ made no such ostentatious display. To the people in general the ceremonies of the mass are both mystifying and awesome. They tend to fill the worshiper with reverential fear. Here is a word picture of the mass as it is performed by the officiating priest. Note carefully the eleven steps in the drama:

"1. The priest first prays with heartfelt sorrow, and profoundly bowing, at the foot of the altar; then having ascended the steps, he kisses it reverently, reads the Introit, and prays again in the spirit of humility to God, by reciting alternately with the server the 'Kyrie eleison' (Lord, have mercy on us). 2. He intones joyfully the Hymn of the Angels (Gloria), and turns then towards the people, to wish them the divine blessing. 3. He prays at the side of the altar, in the name of all who are present, to God for the necessities of all. After that, he reads two portions of the Holy Scripture, the Epistle and the Gospel, the latter, however, at the other side of the altar, to intimate that the evangelical doctrine, rejected by the Jews, passed over to the heathens. 4. The Gospel is followed, on certain days, by the Nicene Creed. This is the preparation for the sacrifice. It was anciently called the *Mass of the Catechumens* – i.e., of those who were still in the first rudiments of Christianity, because they were permitted to assist at it thus far before they were baptized. Next begins, 5. The sacrifice itself by the Offertory: the priest, united with the people, offers bread and wine, and then washes his hands, to show the purity of heart with which we should assist at the holy sacrifice. 6. He invites all to fervent prayer, and, praising God, he joins with the choirs of angels, saying: 'Holy, holy, holy,' etc. 7. Next follow prayers, said in a low voice, for the church, her rulers, and all the faithful, under the invocation of the blessed virgin and all the saints. 8. Then he pronounces the mysterious words of consecration, adores, making a genuflection, and elevates the sacred body and the sacred blood above his head. At the ringing of the bell the people adore on their knees, and strike their breasts in token of repentance for their sins. 9. The priest begs of God graciously to accept the sacrifice, to have mercy on all mankind, also on the souls in purgatory, and concludes with the Lord's Prayer, which contains the substance of all petitions. 10. After a preparatory prayer, during which, at solemn masses, the kiss of peace is given, follows the holy communion of which all those who are present should partake, at least spiritually. 11. The communion being over, the whole concludes with a prayer of thanksgiving, the blessing of the people, and the reading of the Gospel of St. John."[39]

Thus one can see that it is in the mysterious words of consecration that the priest goes to great excesses when he assumes the role of transmuting a wafer (which is made of flour and water, and baked) into the real body of Christ. So says a papal priest:

"The bread and wine, the con secrated stone, a priest, is all that is needed now, for at any moment it is in his power to call the Lord of glory with holy words down upon the earth, to bless Him with his lips, to hold Him in his hands, to receive Him into his mouth, and to distribute Him to the faithful, whilst at the same time the angels stand about him in reverent awe to honour Him who is sacrificed. 'The power of the priest,' exclaims St. Bernardine of Sienna, 'surpasses the power of the blessed virgin; Mary brought the Son of God only once into this world, the priest can do so daily.' The moment of consecration comes, the priest's head is bowed as the awful words fall from his lips: 'This is My body.' With the swiftness of light, the Lord of hosts has 'leaped down from His throne on high,' the substance of the bread has gone, and in his hands, which he has striven to render 'holy and undefiled,' the Melchisedeck of the new law holds his Creator, Redeemer and judge. A moment more and by the second words of consecration, 'This is My blood,' the Lamb of God lies 'mystically slain,' for the sacrifice of Calvary and the altar are the same."[40]

"'Marvelous dignity of priests!' exclaims St. Augustine; 'in their hands, as in the womb of the blessed virgin Mary, the Son of God becomes incarnate.'...Behold the power of

---
39 Deharbe 270, 271.
40 Doyle, 14.

the priest! The tongue of the priest makes God from a morsel of bread! It is more than creating the world. Someone said, 'Does St. Philomena, then, obey the curé of Ars?' Certainly, she may well obey him, since God obeys him. The blessed virgin cannot make her divine Son descend into the host. A priest can, however simple he may be."[41]

The doctrine of transubstantiation, like many other doctrines of the papal church, was a controverted question for centuries before it received final adoption. It was Paschasius Radbertus, a Benedictine monk (786-860), who first advocated the doctrine of the "real presence" (transubstantiation) by the changing of the elements into the "body and blood of Christ." From the publishing of his treatise in A. D. 831 on the "real presence" until the Fourth Lateran Council in A. D. 1215, at which time the doctrine was adopted as a dogma, many fierce verbal battles were fought by the bishops against the teaching of Paschasius.[42]

The question that should come home to us now is, Does the Sacred Bible agree with Paschasianism?

The sacrifice of the mass is not supported by the word of God, although it is the center of Roman Catholic worship.

Let us turn our minds to the upper room where Christ and the twelve disciples were eating the Passover supper. "And when the hour was come, He sat down, and the twelve apostles with Him. And He said unto them, With desire I have desired to eat this passover with you before I suffer." [Luke 22:14, 15]

This was the last valid Passover that was to be kept, for the true Passover Lamb was to die the next afternoon. The slaying of the Passover lamb by the Jews for 1,500 years had pointed to the death of Christ. Desiring to leave a

---

[41] H. Convert, *Eucharistic Meditations* (Extracts from the writings of the blessed J. M. Vianney), (New York: Benziger Brothers, 1923) 111, 112.

[42] "Paschasius Radbertus," *The Catholic Encyclopedia*, v2, 518; Samuel Edgar, *The Variations of Popery*, 10th complete American ed. (New York: S. W. Benedict, 1850) 405–409.

memorial of His death, one that would ever keep in mind the two great events, the fact of His death and the promise of His second coming, Jesus instituted the Lord's Supper.

The unfermented wine and the unleavened bread were on the table. He took the bread and "blessed it," or, as Luke says, "gave thanks," and then broke it, saying, "Take, eat; this is My body." [Matt. 26:26; Luke 22:19] It was Thursday night, according to modern reckoning of the days, when the Lord broke the bread and gave it to His disciples. If it were true that He gave them His real body, then He died that night instead of on the following afternoon of Good Friday. As he did on a previous occasion, Peter would have uttered some word of surprise if Jesus had meant that then He was to suffer and be killed by His own hands. The Lord did not state that He was then taking His own life. [Matthew 16:21, 22] How absurd to think for one moment that Jesus handed them His own flesh to eat! There is more truth than poetry in the words of the old Arabian sage Averroes (died c.1198): "I have traveled over the world, and seen many people; but none so sottish and ridiculous as Christians, who devour the God they worship."[43]

The Roman Catholic Church claims that by the statement, "This is My body," is meant the *real* body of Christ. But there are other texts in the Holy Bible that mention the body of Christ. For instance, the church is called the "body of Christ." [Eph. 4:12; 1:22, 23] No one could ever be mistaken here as to the meaning of the term: "He is the head of the body, the church." [Colossians 1:18]

According to the reasoning of the papal church on the words "This is My body," one can just as logically hold that in the service of the mass the people who comprise the church are transmuted into the wafer as the real body and blood of Christ.

---

[43] *The Variations of Popery*, 10th complete American ed., 421. Quoting Averroes.

The Mass

Christ, when He spoke of Himself as being the bread, was not teaching the doctrine of transubstantiation. It is absurd to charge the Son of God with creating Himself out of a literal piece of bread. If what the Roman Catholic Church teaches were true concerning Christ's use of the term "bread," would it not equally apply to the other words by which He referred to Himself, such as "the door," [John 10:9] "the vine," [John 15:1] "the light," [John 8:12] "the root," [Rev. 22:16] "the rock," [1 Cor. 10:4] and "the bright and morning star"? [Rev. 22:16] If we apply the logic of the papacy for interpreting Christ's statement, "I am that bread of life," [John 6:48] is it not possible by the same mode of interpretation to say that Christ is changed into a door, a vine, a light, a root, a rock, and a star? It if holds good in one instance, it must of necessity hold good in others.

The bread that the Roman Catholic Church gives to her laity is not broken. It is a round, disk-shaped wafer, that is served completely whole. By thus administering the wafer whole, they spoil the import of the figure which Jesus left to represent His broken body. He *broke* the bread when He gave it to His disciples.

Why the roundness of the wafer, it may be asked. Moses, who was instructed by God to tell the Hebrews to prepare the unleavened bread for the Passover feast, has left nothing on record to indicate the form or shape of the bread. The question may arise, Where did the thin, round wafer of the papal mass originate? It probably came from sun worship. "Almost every jot or tittle in the Egyptian worship had a symbolical meaning. The *round disk*, so frequent in the sacred emblems of Egypt, symbolized the *sun*."[44] Our Lord was careful to guard His people from: anything that would relate to sun worship. He regarded sun worship as a "greater" abomination than the other

---

44　Alexander Hislop, *The Two Babylons* (1905, reprint, Brushton, New York: TEACH Services, Inc., 2002) 160.

forms of idolatry committed by the Israelites. [Ezekiel 8:3, 16] Would the Lord permit the sacred ordinance given as a memorial of His Son's death to be copied from pagan worship? Never!

The giving of the cup is an essential part of the Lord's Supper. "And He took the cup, and gave, thanks, and gave it to them, saying, Drink ye all of it." [Matt. 26:27] Here it is stated that Jesus gave thanks as He passed to His disciples the cup. Can we fancy Jesus giving them His own real blood to drink? Would they not be counted among the rankest of cannibals, by drinking the blood of their divine Redeemer? Nevertheless, we have this statement: "The [Roman] Catholic Church has always believed and taught that Jesus gave the apostles His true and real body and blood."[45] Such teaching is not in harmony with the Bible. Let us now see what the Sacred Scriptures say, whether or not it is a case of transubstantiation or one of commemoration.

"And He [Christ] took bread, and gave thanks, and brake it, and gave unto them, saying, This is My body which is given for you: this do in remembrance of Me." [Luke 22:19] The word "remembrance" is given in the Douay Version, as "commemoration." In their revised New Testament the term "remembrance" is used by the Roman Catholic translators. Therefore, the Lord's Supper was instituted as a reminder, or memorial, of the great sacrifice of Jesus Christ, just as the seventh-day Sabbath is the memorial of the creation of the world by God. Twice in the following texts the apostle Paul quotes Christ as saying that the communion service was instituted "in remembrance" of Himself. "For I have received of the Lord that which also I delivered unto you, That the Lord Jesus the same night in which He was betrayed took bread: and when He had given thanks, He brake it, and said, Take, eat:

---
[45] Butler, 241.

this is My body, which is broken for you: this do *in remembrance* of Me. After the same manner also He took the cup, when He had supped, saying, This cup is the new testament in My blood: this do ye, as oft as ye drink it, *in remembrance* of Me." [1 Cor. 11:23-25] It not only points backward to His death but also points forward to His second coming.

The wine used by Christ at the Last Supper was unfermented. "But I say unto you, I will not drink henceforth of this fruit of the vine, until that day when I drink it new with you in My Father's kingdom." [Matt. 26:29] Why was it the "fruit of the vine"? Because ferment is a type of sin, and as there was "no sin" in the life of the Son of God; so the wine, which represented His blood, must be without ferment. It was "the pure blood of the grape," in which there was a blessing. [Deut. 32:14; Isa. 65:8] The bread used was unleavened, like that used at the Passover feast. [Exod. 12:8, 15, 18, 39; Num. 9:11] Leaven, like ferment, is a type of sin, as Paul clearly points out: "Purge out therefore the old leaven, that ye may be a new lump, as ye are unleavened. For even Christ our passover is sacrificed for us: therefore let us keep the feast, not with old leaven, neither with the leaven of malice and wickedness; but with the unleavened bread of sincerity and truth." [1 Cor. 5:7, 8]

The Roman Catholic Church uses the unleavened bread, but the wine which she uses is fermented. By so doing she makes it appear as though there were sin in the life of Christ. Some Protestant churches use leavened bread and unfermented wine.

The repetition of the mass is another thing that strikes at the very heart of the atonement which Christ made on the cross. If the following statements are true, Christ is continually sacrificed on the altars of the Roman Catholic Church. The teaching of this church is thus:

"On the altars of the [Roman] Catholic Church, whose zone of chalices encircles the world, the mass is celebrated

The Wine of Roman Babylon

every day. Since time changes from continent to continent, this morning sacrifice is at every moment, taking place somewhere."[46]

"The world, in fact, since the redemption, is an immense temple where at each moment of time, as the sun advances over a hemisphere, the Victim of Calvary is uplifted between heaven and earth by thousands of priests, to the glory of the Most High....After the consecration, the good God is there as in heaven!"[47]

Does the Book of God furnish any light on this matter? Yes, the Lord, who knew that such a doctrine would be propagated, has made every provision to refute it. "So Christ was *once* offered to bear the sins of many; and unto them that look for Him shall He appear the second time without sin unto salvation." [Heb. 9:28] "Note that"Christ was *once* offered." That *once* was sufficient to atone for the sins of the whole human family, for "we are sanctified through the offering of the body of Jesus Christ *once for all*."[48]

The priests that offer "oftentimes the same sacrifice," God declares, can never take away sin. "And every priest standeth daily ministering and offering oftentimes the same sacrifices, which can never take away sins: but this man, after He had offered *one* sacrifice for sins *forever*, sat down on the right hand of God....For by *one* offering He hath perfected for ever them that are sanctified." [Heb.

---

46 Charles A. Martin, *Catholic Religion*, popular ed., (St. Louis, B. Herder Book Co., 1919) 195.
47 Convert, 116.
48 Hebrews 10:10. *Note*: This does not mean "once for all" men, but once for all time. The phrase "once for all" is a translation of the Greek adverb *ephapax*, which means "once." It is used five times in the New Testament. (Romans 6:10; 1 Corinthians 15:6; Hebrews 7:27; 9:12; 10:10.) In Hebrews 10:10 the apostle uses the term in the sense of "once for all" because he contrasts the sufficiency of the sacrifice of Christ with the sacrifices offered *daily* (verse 11) by the priest of the Hebrew priesthood. The revised Roman Catholic New Testament says in Hebrews 10:10 that "we have been sanctified through the offering of the body of Jesus Christ once for all."

10:11-14] Christ, after He had offered one sacrifice for sin, "sat down."[49] The priests of the Roman Catholic Church teach that they bring Christ down each time that mass is offered.

The following text is sufficient to refute all claims of the act of transubstantiation: "I am He that liveth, and was dead; and, behold, *I am alive for evermore.*"[50] He is alive *for evermore.* No human being has the power to put Christ to death again. Paul speaks of Christians as "knowing that Christ being raised from the dead dieth no more; death hath no more dominion over Him. For in that He died, He died unto sin *once.*"[51] Christ has been raised from the dead, and the Divine Word says that He "dieth no more; death hath no more dominion over Him." Christ has gone beyond the power and dominion of man to sacrifice Him, and death cannot touch Him.

"When Jesus therefore had received the vinegar, He said, It is finished: and He bowed His head, and gave up the ghost." [John 19:30] On the cross Jesus said, "It is finished." Thus He acknowledged before the universe that His sacrifice was complete, "for by one offering He hath perfected forever them that are sanctified." [Hebrews 10:14] "One offering" is all that is necessary for our perfection.

According to the evidence here submitted from the Holy Scriptures, it is beyond the power of human beings to take Christ from heaven and put Him to death by sacrifice. Every spark of human feeling left in our being recoils at the

---

[49] The revised Roman Catholic New Testament says: "Jesus, having offered one sacrifice for sins, *has taken His seat forever at the right* hand of God....For by *one* offering He has perfected forever those who are sanctified."

[50] Revelation 1:18. The revised Roman Catholic New testament reads: "I am living forevermore."

[51] Romans 6:9, 10. The revised Roman Catholic New Testament says: "we know that christ, having risen from the dead, *dies now no more*, Death shall no longer have dominion over Him. For the death that He died, He died to sin once for all."

very thought of putting our blessed Lord to death again. The doctrine of transubstantiation never should have become a church dogma. It is an error and is devoid of support from the Written Word of divine revelation. It strikes at the very foundation of the plan of salvation, and depreciates the value of the supreme sacrifice of Christ on the cross.

At a certain part of the mass the wafer, which the priest claims is the real Christ, is elevated or held up before the congregation to be worshiped. Soon after the doctrine of transubstantiation was indorsed at the Fourth Lateran Council, in A. D. 1215, by Innocent III, the elevation of the host (from Latin, *hostia*, meaning "victim at a certain part of the mass, was introduced by Honorius III. After the priest has pronounced the mysterious words "*Hoc est corpus meum*" (This is My Body), he elevates the host. At this juncture, when the altar boy rings the bell, the people fall on their knees and adore the consecrated wafer. The following quotation clearly reveals this doctrine:

> "Then he [the priest] pronounces the mysterious words of consecration, adores, making a genuflection, and elevates the sacred body and the sacred blood above his head. At the ringing of the bell the people adore on their knees, and strike their breasts in token of repentance for their sins."[52]

Such adoration paid to a wafer-god is really idolatry. God says: "Thou shalt not make unto thee any graven image, or any likeness of anything that is in heaven above, or that is in the earth beneath, or that is in the water under the earth: thou shalt not bow down thyself to them, nor serve them: for I the Lord thy God am a jealous God, visiting the iniquity of the fathers upon the children unto the third and fourth generation of them that hate Me, and showing mercy unto thousands of them that love Me, and keep My commandments." [Exod. 20:4, 5]

---

[52] Deharbe, 270.

The Mass

The Lord never intended to have His Son fashioned into a wafer or any other object and worshiped. God asks this question: "To whom then will ye liken God? Or what likeness will ye compare unto Him?" [Isa. 40:18] Is there anything fashioned by man that can be likened to Jesus? Nothing! "Forasmuch then as we are the offspring of God, we ought not to think that the Godhead is like unto gold, or silver, or stone, graven by art and man's device." [Acts 17:29] Man has sought out many ways to fashion objects for worship, but in the case of the mass it takes only a few Latin words spoken by a priest to make the wafer the veritable center of the papist's devotion. He says: "The tongue of the priest makes God from a morsel of bread."[53] If the Godhead cannot be likened to pure metal such as gold and silver, surely He cannot be likened to "a morsel of bread."

Thus we can clearly see that the papal sacrament of the mass is not supported by the Sacred Scriptures. The mass exerts an enchanting influence upon those who participate in it. Knowing what Holy Writ teaches concerning the holy communion, why should anyone hesitate to refrain from further sipping from Babylon's cup of error?

Also see the Appendix p. 203.

---

53   Convert, *112.*

Romanism is a religion of much outward show. The procession, staged in San Francisco, shows pilgrims parading solemnly through the streets. Flanked by priests, acolytes, and a uniformed guard of honor, Thomas A. Connoly, auxiliary bishop of San Francisco, carries the sacrament as he walks beneath a white and gold canopy. (Photo by Religious News Service.)

CHAPTER VII

Omission of the Cup

THE SIXTH sip from the golden cup of Babylon, which should not be overlooked, is "Omission of the Cup." This restriction of the use of the wine of the communion to the priests came in at the Council of Constance (A.D. 1414-1418), was confirmed by the Council of Basle (A.D. 1431), and reaffirmed by the Council of Trent (A.D. 1545-1563). Turning to the Sacred Scriptures and examining them on the subject of the celebration of the Lord's Supper, one finds that both emblems — the bread and the wine — are to be partaken of by the laity as well as by the ministers who officiate in the service. This is a vital point, one which should be studied carefully and prayerfully by all devout Roman Catholics. The communicants of the papal church are never permitted to partake of the cup at the altar, although the priest himself partakes of both the bread and the wine.

The unquestionable authority is the word of God, to which one must resort in order to know whether or not the omission of the sacramental cup is a correct procedure. In the Gospel of Mark it is clear that Jesus, on instituting the Lord's Supper, gave the cup and "they all drank of it." [Mark 14:23] The withholding of the wine from the laity is unscriptural, as acknowledged by Leo the Great, who said in 443 that the omission of the cup is "sacrilegious dissimulation."[54]

---

[54] Leo the Great, quoted by Samuel Edgar, *The Variations of Popery*, 430, 431.

The Wine of Roman Babylon

In the study of this subject one finds that several Roman bishops were very much opposed to the introduction of this doctrine. Gelasius I, Urban II, Paschal II, and others raised their voices in protest against it, and despite the fact that even the General Council of Constance (A.D. 1414–1418), in its thirteenth session, admitted that the primitive church partook of both the bread and the wine in the communion service,[55] this omission of the cup was introduced and has long since been adopted.

The withholding of the cup from the laity is diametrically opposed to the teaching of the word of God, as is clearly set forth in the following texts: "For I have received of the Lord that which also I delivered unto you, That the Lord Jesus the same night in which He was betrayed took bread: and when He had given thanks, He brake it, and said, Take, eat; this is My body, which is broken for you: this do in remembrance of Me. After the same manner also lie took the cup, when He had supped, saying, This cup is the new testament in My blood: this do ye, as oft as ye drink it, in remembrance of Me." [1 Cor. 11:23–25]

If either of the emblems were to be suspended, it should have been the bread, because more is said about the blood than concerning the body of the Lord. The following texts show how much importance is placed upon the blood of Christ: "Forasmuch as ye know that ye were not redeemed with corruptible things,...but with the precious blood of Christ." [1 Pet. 1:18, 19] "And [they] have washed their robes, and made them white in the blood of the Lamb." [Rev. 7:14] "Being now justified by His blood, we shall be saved." [Rom. 5:9] "And they overcame him by the blood of the Lamb." [Rev. 12:11]

To omit the cup from the communion service is to strike at the very heart of the atonement made by Christ. The following renderings of various versions of Matthew 26:27

---

55   See Samuel Edgar, ibid., 432, 433.

give us unmistakable evidence that the Lord intended that no one should be denied the privilege of partaking of the cup.

"And taking a cup, He gave thanks and gave it to them, saying, 'All of you drink of this.'" (Revised Roman Catholic New Testament.)

"Then He took a cup, and offered thanks, and gave it to them, saying, Drink, all of you, of this." (R. A. Knox, Roman Catholic.)

"And He took the cup, and offered thanks; and gave [it] to them, saying: Take, drink of this all of you." (Murdock's translation from the Syriac.)

"He also took a cup and after thanking God He gave it to them saying, Drink of it, all of you." (Moffatt.)

"And He took a cup, and gave thanks, and gave to them, saying, Drink of it, all of you." (American Baptist Improved.)

"And having taken the cup, and given thanks, He gave to them, saying, Drink ye of it—all." (Young.)

"And taking a cup and giving thanks, He gave unto them, saying, Drink of it all of you." (The Emphasized Bible, Rotherham.)

"And He took the wine-cup and gave thanks and gave it to them, saying, 'You must all drink from it.'" (Goodspeed.)

"Then He took a cup, and after saying the thanksgiving, gave it to them, with the words: 'Drink from it, all of you.'" (Twentieth Century New Testament.)

"And He took the cup and gave thanks, and gave it to them saying, 'Drink from it, all of you.'" (Weymouth.)

"And taking the cup and giving thanks, He gives it to them, saying, 'All drink of it.'" (Concordant.)

The Wine of Roman Babylon

"And taking the chalice, He gave thanks, and gave to them, saying: Drink ye all of this." (Douay.)

Love for Jesus and His precious word ought to constrain all to follow His instruction by partaking of both the sacramental cup and the bread, and to refuse. to be influenced by the decrees laid down by the church councils that legislate contrary to the teachings of Holy Writ.

Also see the Appendix p. 205.

CHAPTER VIII

Masses and Purgatory

THE SEVENTH sip of the wine of Babylon we shall name "Barter in Masses and Purgatory." The Roman Catholic Church teaches that the sacrifice of the mass, as offered by the priest, serves as a propitiation for sin, and is also a means of obtaining graces and blessings from God. The following quotations reveal the position which that church holds respecting the efficacy of the mass to liberate souls from the fires of purgatory:

"Christian revelation teaches us that besides heaven into which no imperfection can enter, and hell from which there is no redemption, there is a state in which the souls of the just who in this life were not perfectly cleansed, shall undergo purifying suffering before being admitted into heaven. This state of purgation is properly called purgatory. The defined teaching of the church is expressed in the words of the Council of Trent: 'That there is a purgatory and that the souls detained there are benefitted by the prayers of the faithful and especially by the acceptable sacrifice of the altar.'...

"The souls who go to purgatory are saved. They are certain of heaven, and shall reach it as soon as they are prepared for it. Purgatory has been called the vestibule of heaven. The power to merit has passed with the time of probation. In purgatory the souls can themselves wipe out their debt only by suffering. Yet purgatory speaks of forgiveness as well as penalty:—of penalty on the part of those who suffer there; of forgiveness on the part of God who is moved by the prayers and good works of the living to remit that penalty either wholly or in part."[56]

---
56   Martin, 288-290.

The Wine of Roman Babylon

"All the souls in purgatory have died in the love of God, and are certain to enter heaven. But as yet they are not pure and holy enough to see God, and God's mercy allots them a place and a time for cleansing and preparation."[57]

"There are souls condemned to burn in purgatory till the day of judgment."[58]

"How long are the souls in purgatory? How long will you be there? Let us give to each venial sin one day in purgatory, and suppose that each day you commit 30 faults. Therefore, to every day of your life 30 days in purgatory will answer: to every year, 30 years; to 50, 1,500 years; to 60, 1,800. Immortal God, what an astonishing payment! Add to the venial sins some mortal sin, absolved indeed, as far as the guilt goes, but not paid for entirely as far as punishment goes. How many other centuries of years in purgatory!"[59]

Many Roman Catholic writers admit that the doctrine of purgatory is not taught in the Bible:

"We would appeal to those general principles of Scripture rather than to particular texts often alleged in proof of purgatory. We doubt if they contain an explicit and direct reference to it."[60]

Cardinal Wiseman admits that a Roman Catholic "could not discover in it [the Bible] one word of purgatory."[61]

This doctrine of purgatory is used to hold the communicants of the papal church in abject fear as well as to enlarge its coffers, as the following shows:

"Look back to the bedside of death. You clasped a hand and said, 'I'll remember you always.' When the life of your mother or father or friend had just reached its course, in that

---

[57] Wm. E. Addis and Thomas Arnold, "Purgatory," *A Catholic Dictionary*, 702.
[58] Cardinal Robert Bellarmine, in Abbe Cloquet, *The Month of the Dead* (New York: Benziger Brothers, 1886) 63.
[59] Esther Muzzarelli, *Month of Mary* (London: Burns and Oates, 1849) 75.
[60] Wm. E. Addis and Thomas Arnold, 704.
[61] Cardinal Nicholas Wiseman, *Lecture on the Principal Doctrines and Practices of the Catholic Church* (Baltimore: J. Murphy, 1846) 6.

most solemn, most weighty of man's moments, you promised you would be faithful. What is the efficacy of that promise now? Is that same soul still waiting at another Pool of Bethsaida for the movement of the waters?

"Could we see these dear souls in purgatory we would not forget them. They cry out in thirst while we sit and drink. They are weary with restlessness while we do be sleeping. They are sore with grievous pain while we are playing. They are eaten up with burning fire while we are feasting. They cry out for help from those who once held them dear. They plead that you have the pity, the prayers, the sacrifices that you promised.

"By prayer we temper the agonies of the souls in purgatory. We hasten their liberation by sacrifice. What are we as individuals doing for our dead? It is one of the mysteries of life that we forget so easily those who have gone before us, when to remember them where remembrance is most efficacious is at the disposal of us all. In the words of the Council of Trent, 'There is a purgatory and the souls there detained are assisted by the suffrages of the faithful, especially by the most acceptable sacrifice of the altar.' Let us remember our dead at mass. Let us have masses said for them."[62]

If words mean anything, such an appeal surely touches the heart of the most adamant person. Who would not be willing to make any sacrifice possible to have masses offered, if they would temper the fires and lessen the period of suffering of the departed loved one? Is it not cruel of that church to take advantage of any one in the hour of his bereavement?

The uncertainties which are attached to the efficacy and validity of the mass is also something to awaken serious thought:

"All masses and prayers for the dead," says one writer, "are applied 'by way of suffrage' — that is, are dependent on God's secret mercy and will, who in His infinite justice may apply to another soul altogether the masses said for a certain

---

[62] *The Jesuit Seminary News* 3:9 (Nov 15, 1928), 70.

The Wine of Roman Babylon

individual. Non-Catholics generally think that 500 masses have 500 times the efficacy of one. This is not the case. The value of each mass is infinite, but we never know with perfect certainty whether or not God has applied it to the individual soul for whom it has been offered, although we do know He answers all our prayers."[63]

A still further authentic statement on this point is: "No one can be certain, with the certainty of faith, that he receives a true sacrament, because the sacrament cannot be valid without the intention of the minister, and no man can see another's intention."[64]

While theologians may deal in uncertainties, the Lord does not. With our immutable God there is "no variableness, neither shadow of turning." [James 1:17]

Christ never repels any poor soul who needs His help. "All that the Father giveth Me shall come to Me; and him that cometh to Me I will in no wise cast out." [John 6:37] No matter how far souls may have drifted in the ocean of sin, Christ "is able also to save them to the uttermost." [Heb. 7:25] Yes, without the aid of money or suffrage of any human being, whether priest or lay member. The invitation which the Lord gives in the following scripture is addressed to both rich and poor alike. "Ho, everyone that thirsteth, come ye to the waters, and he that hath no money; come ye, buy, and eat; yea, come, buy wine and milk without money and without price." [Isa.55:1] The poor as well as the rich may be the recipients of God's grace.

Salvation is a "free gift," bestowed on the merits of Jesus Christ. Since it is a gift, it is therefore something that cannot be purchased. "The gift of God is eternal life through Jesus Christ our Lord." [Rom. 6:23] When offered money for the

---

[63] Conway, 325.
[64] Cardinal Robert Bellarmine, *De Justificatione*, Bk. 3, chap. 8. In his *Disputationes de Controversiis Christianae Fidei adversus Hujus Temporis Haereticos*, v4, p442, col. 2.

gift of the Holy Spirit, Peter refused to accept it and rebuked Simon severely for thinking that the favor of God could be purchased with money. "But Peter said unto him, Thy money perish with thee, because thou hast thought that the gift of God may be purchased with money. Thou hast neither part nor lot in this matter: for thy heart is not right in the sight of God. Repent therefore of this thy wickedness and pray God, if perhaps the thought of thine heart may be forgiven thee. For I perceive that thou art in the gall of bitterness, and in the bond of iniquity." [Acts 8:20-23]

How wonderful it would be if those who profess to be followers of Peter would pursue a similar course! If they did, traffic in masses and the sale of indulgences would soon disappear. If the purchasing of the favor of God was not permitted for the living in the days of the apostles, how can we conceive of its being allowed now in behalf of the dead, whose probation is ended? Money can secure many things in this life, but Christ assures us that it will avail nothing in the hereafter. "Then said Jesus unto His disciples, Verily I say unto you, That a rich man shall hardly enter into the kingdom of heaven....It is easier for a camel to go through the eye of a needle, than for a rich man to enter into the kingdom of God." [Matt. 19:23, 24]

As Christ taught the people, He made it very plain that a person possessing great riches does not have any premium on heaven. If the Lord intended that the offering of masses (which involves the payment of money) for the liberation of souls from the penalties of sin could save men, He never would have made this statement about the man who is rich. On the contrary, He would have recommended riches as a means of obtaining salvation. According to the papal doctrine, Roman Catholics have their credit in eternal rewards. Inasmuch as money plays such a part in the stipend, or tax, fixed by the bishop for the celebration of the mass, it naturally would be a great advantage to have such sums as are necessary to meet the demands, so that the special fruits of a larger number of masses could be obtained.

The dreadful description of the torments endured by those who are confined to the imaginary fires of the purgatorial regions is constantly kept before the devout of the papal church by designing priests. The terror that is awakened induces the listeners to leave nothing untried to shorten their period of suffering in purgatory, and, if possible, to escape it altogether. Time has not effaced the indelible impression made upon my mind by what I heard while attending a mission at my parish church. The presiding monk stressed the point of failing to confess mortal as well as venial sins to the priest, and told the following story:

A young lady, in company with her brother, committed a sin. What the sin was, he failed to say. (This no doubt was purposely omitted so as to make the hearer wonder if he had perhaps committed the same sin.) The brother confessed the sin to the priest and received absolution. The sister, however, did not. The withholding of confession is sometimes due to fear. Shortly after, she took ill, and no cure could be found for her malady. She was supposed to be suffering under divine retribution. just as life was ebbing away, she began all at once to tear the hair out of her head, her eyes glared as balls of fire, and her tongue protruded out of her mouth. In desperation her family called the priest. As he entered the room, she exclaimed: "Away with you, holy father! I am already damned, for the gates of hell now are opened to me, and I can feel the tortures of the inferno to which I am to be confined forever and ever!"

Listening to such teaching, my youthful mind could not conceive of God as a loving father, or of Christ as having died for my sins because He *loved* me. God was pictured as

Masses and Purgatory

a tyrant ever seeking to execute vengeance upon all who were guilty of mortal sin. So fearful was I that I might fail to confess to the priest all my sins and consequently be confined at death to the fires of purgatory or hell, that I wished a thousand times I had never been born. Only those who have passed through the experience can understand what fear and suffering harrass the mind of the devout Roman Catholic. The only remedy for a sinsick soul is to be taught and led by God's word as found in the Sacred Bible, and the only way that real peace can be assured is by keeping His commandments with the help of the grace of Christ. "Thus saith the Lord, thy Redeemer, the Holy One of Israel; I am the Lord thy God which teacheth thee to profit, which leadeth thee by the way that thou shouldest go. O that thou hadst hearkened to My commandments! Then had thy peace been as a river, and thy righteousness as the waves of the sea." [Isa. 48:17, 18]

Instead of seeking God with contrition of heart and asking for power to live in obedience to the Ten Commandments, the one burdened with sins is taught by Romanism to seek plenary indulgence, to resort to pilgrimages, and to appeal to everything that the human mind can devise for the purpose of expiating sins. Can any human effort erase the stain of sin from a guilty soul? "For though thou wash thee with nitre, and take thee much soap, yet thine iniquity is marked before Me, saith the Lord God." [Jer. 2:22] If fire, or chemicals, could cleanse a soul from the defilement of sin, it would not have been necessary for Christ to have died. The papal purging by fire after death annuls the complete atonement which was made by Christ. "If we confess our sins, He is faithful and just to forgive us our sins, and to cleanse us from all unrighteousness." What has God provided to cleanse us from all sins? [1 John 1:19] "The blood of Jesus Christ His Son cleanseth us from all sin." [1 John 1:7]

Thus it is the blood of Christ, and not the fire of a purgatory, that purifies a soul for heaven. These texts should settle forever the question concerning venial sins, which are the lesser evils, and for which souls are consigned to purgatory to be purged by burning. It is always a puzzling question to many to differentiate between venial sins and mortal sins. It is the mortal sins that the priest forgives in confession. Papal doctrine holds that if they are not confessed, the one who commits them is doomed to the fires of hell, out of which there is no redemption. God declares that "all unrighteousness is sin," and He does not divide evil deeds into mortal and venial sins. Although we have a God who does not condone sin in any of us, regardless of its character, He gives us the tender invitation to come and reason together with Him (not to the priest, and not to the confessional, but where we may be), with the assurance that though your sins be as scarlet, they shall be as white as snow; though they be red like crimson, they shall be as wool. [Isa. 1:18]

It is while we are living that the invitation to come to the Lord holds good, not when we are dead, for He says: "They that go down into the pit cannot hope for Thy truth." [Isa. 38:18] "The dead know not anything." [Eccles. 9:5]

The parable of the prodigal son [Luke 15:11–24] was given by Christ for the purpose of showing the utter depravity of the human heart. Sinful man has nothing to satisfy the just claims of God's broken law; his filthy rags [Isa. 64:6] must be exchanged for the white raiment [Rev. 3:5, 18; 19:8] woven in the loom of heaven. Were it not for our heavenly Father's love and tender mercy, the prodigal would never be accepted as a son. How happy and appreciative we should be for the provision there is in the gospel of Jesus Christ for our salvation without the meritorious works imposed by doctrines and commandments of men.

In summing up the evidence from the Holy Scriptures, we find that the traffic in masses should be expunged and forever debarred from the belief of all Christian communicants, The Lord desires to have His people accept His plan of salvation in its entirety; and He would have those who have tarried at the Babylonian cup stop imbibing its mysterious brew.

Also see the Appendix p. 207.

The flickering candles, the ornate images, the richly colored vestments, the solemn movements of the priests, the smell of burning incense, and the lights and shadows in the building itself are all designed to captivate the senses of the mass, the supreme act of Roman Catholic worship. The picture shows Archbishop Spellman of New York celebrating an Easter mass in St. Patrick's Cathedral. (Photo by Acme.)

CHAPTER IX

Peter and the Rock

THE EIGHTH sip, "Peter and the Rock," issuing from the Babylonish cup is next to be considered and tested by the Holy Scriptures. Laying aside all prejudices, let us examine cautiously what the Roman Catholic Church teaches concerning its leader. It is this doctrine, above all others, that has caused Roman Catholics to rest securely in the belief that theirs is the only true church, because it is supposed to have been founded upon Peter. To show the position the Roman Catholic Church teaches on this point, let us note a statement taken from the works of Cardinal Gibbons:

"Jesus, our Lord, founded but one church, which He was pleased to build on Peter. Therefore, any church that does not recognize Peter as its foundation stone is not the church of Christ, and therefore cannot stand, for it is not the work of God."[65]

Another well-known papal authority gives the following information relative to that church's teaching concerning the primacy of Peter:

"In especially solemn fashion Christ accentuated Peter's precedence among the apostles, when, after Peter had recognized Him as the Messias, He promised that he would be head of His flock....By the word 'rock' the Saviour cannot have meant Himself, but only Peter....His statement then admits of but one explanation, namely, that He wishes to make Peter the head of the whole community of those who believed in Him as the true Messias; that through this

---

[65] Gibbons, 100.

The Wine of Roman Babylon

foundation (Peter) the kingdom of Christ would be unconquerable; that the spiritual guidance of the faithful was placed in the hands of Peter, as the special representative of Christ. This meaning becomes so much the clearer when we remember that the words 'bind' and 'loose' are not metaphorical, but Jewish juridical terms. It is also clear that the position of Peter among the other apostles and in the Christian community was the basis for the kingdom of God on earth, that is, the church of Christ. Peter was personally installed as head of the apostles by Christ Himself. This foundation created for the church by its Founder could not disappear with the person of Peter, but was intended to continue and did continue (as actual history shows) in the primacy of the Roman Church and its bishops."[66]

The words spoken to Peter are familiar to every devout Roman Catholic, and are often cited to support their claim that Peter is the rock. What caused the Son of God to make this declaration to Peter? Did He intend to set a precedent by elevating a human agent to the position of head of His universal church? It is necessary in discovering the meaning of any terms used symbolically or relatively to find the antecedent. The Divine Record gives the context of the use of the term "rock" as follows:

"When Jesus came into the coasts of Caesarea Philippi, He asked His disciples, saying, Whom do men say that I the Son of man am? And they said, Some say that Thou art John the Baptist: some, Elias; and others, Jeremias, or one of the prophets. He saith unto them, But whom say ye that I am? And Simon Peter answered and said, Thou art the Christ, the Son of the living God. And Jesus answered and said unto him, Blessed art thou, Simon Barjona: for flesh and blood hath not revealed it unto thee, but My Father which is in heaven. And I say also unto thee, That thou art Peter, and upon this rock I will build My church; and the gates of hell shall not prevail against it." [Matt. 16:13-18]

---

[66] "Peter," *The Catholic Encyclopedia* v2, 745, 746.

Peter and the Rock

On the return of the disciples, who had been out on a missionary tour, Jesus desired to know whether the people regarded Him as the Son of God or as an ordinary man. Hence He said to them: "Whom do men say that I the Son of man am?" How disappointed He must have been as He listened to the testimonies that they brought back, seeing that some believed Him to be John the Baptist, others thought He was Elijah, and still others held that He was Jeremiah. These were all good men, indeed, but they were not able to save a lost world. Were the disciples influenced in any way by the opinions of the people? Did they come back weakened in their faith as to the divinity of Christ?

Jesus, desiring an expression of their faith on this vital question, asked them, "But whom say ye that I am?" The impulsive Peter spoke for himself and the rest of the disciples, and answered: "Thou art the Christ, the Son of the living God." Thus he recognized that Jesus was more than an ordinary man. Upon Christ, whom Peter confessed to be the Son of God, would be built His church. This glorious confession of faith by Peter called forth a divine benediction from Christ, who said, "Blessed art thou, Simon Bar-jona: for flesh and blood hath not revealed it unto thee, but My Father which is in heaven." There is a tendency on the part of the human to become lifted up, particularly when words of commendation are uttered by one who is his superior. Jesus, knowing Peter's weakness and desiring to safeguard him against assuming an air of superiority, attributed the truth the apostle uttered not to his own mind but to a revelation coming directly from God.

Prior to Peter's acknowledgment of Christ's divinity, the other disciples had openly expressed their belief in Christ as the Son of God. In the night of terror when the disciples were in the boat tossed about on the angry waves, joy filled their hearts upon seeing their Saviour walking on the foaming sea. After Peter had walked on the waves to meet his Lord and had returned, the eleven exclaimed to their Master: "Of a truth Thou art the Son of God." [Matt. 14:28–33]

If the mere acknowledgment by Peter that Christ was the Son of God would suffice for him to be the foundation rock of the church, it would be reasonable to conclude that the same honor should be conferred upon the other disciples, for they, too, confessed the divinity of Christ. If the primacy was given to Peter, as stated by the Roman Catholic Church, because of his recognition of Christ as the Divine One, then the Lord, who is no respecter of persons, ought to have given a similar reward to the other disciples.

The Roman Catholic Church's doctrine on this important subject is entirely foreign to the thought which Christ intended to convey, when He said: "Thou art Peter, and upon this rock I will build My church; and the gates of hell shall not prevail against it." Could it be that this massive superstructure, the church of God, has for its foundation a weak, vacillating character such as was Peter? Very, very soon after the words of Christ were uttered to Peter, the Master was obliged to rebuke him for trying to dissuade Him from following the path of duty. "But be turned, and said unto Peter, Get thee behind Me, Satan: thou art an offense unto Me: for thou savourest not the things that be of God, but those that be of men." [Matt. 16:23] This scathing rebuke was certainly not indicative of the ecclesiastical dignity and primacy which the papists attribute to Peter.

The Romanists maintain that the terms "Peter" and "rock" in Matthew 16:18 mean one and the same thing. Let us note carefully the Lord's statement. "Thou art Peter, and upon this rock I will build My church; and the gates of hell shall not prevail against it." The name "Peter" in the original text is *petros*, a Greek word meaning "a stone" (a rolling stone); and the Greek word for "rock" is *petra*, which means "a rock" of large dimensions. For example, we have the word *petra* used twice in Matthew 7:24, 25 to

Peter and the Rock

mean a foundation rock. But in Matthew 13:5, 20 and Mark 4: 16 we read that some of the seed fell upon *ta petrode* (in Mark 4: 5, *to petrodes*), the "stony ground" formed by many a *petros* (rolling stone). Moreover, the Greek word *petros* (translated in Matthew 16:18 as "Peter") is a masculine noun, whereas *petra* (rendered "rock" in Matthew 16: 8) is a feminine substantive.

The Book of God states that His church is made up of spiritual, living stones. [1 Pet. 2:5] Consequently Peter, whose name means "a stone," was one of them, as every other Christian is. Peter, who was a rough stone taken from the quarry of the world and hewed and polished by trials and tests, found his place in that spiritual building. Everyone will have to go through this chiseling and polishing process to be fitted for a place in Christ's "spiritual house." There is quite a contrast between the words *petros* and *petra*, just as there is a vast difference between a movable stone and an immovable rock. Peter truly was a movable stone, and he was so far removed from his Lord that he denied Him by cursing and swearing. [Matt. 26:58, 69–75; Mark 14:54, 66–72] The Omnipotent One was too wise to establish His church solely upon such an unstable and inconstant character as Peter.

Truly, the gates of hell did prevail against Peter, and they will prevail against a church or a human being who has for its foundation such human material as was demonstrated in the life of that apostle. Even Paul, many years later, had to rebuke Peter because he and Barnabas "walked not uprightly according to the truth of the gospel." [Gal. 2:11–14] He was compelling "the Gentiles to live as do the Jews." But there is security in the church which has for her foundation Christ Himself, the One who set His face like a flint [Isa. 50:7] and who was not moved, though the blasts and storms of the enemy beat furiously upon Him. Christ, the Mighty Petra, is the true foundation, and the gates of hell have never prevailed against Him. He declares: "Whosoever heareth these sayings of Mine, and doeth them, I will liken him unto a wise man, which built his house upon a rock [*petra*]: and the rain descended, and the floods came, and the winds blew, and beat upon that house; and it fell not: for it was founded upon a rock [*petra*]." [Matt. 7:24, 25]

Moses, who talked with God face to face, and whose writings Jesus repeatedly endorsed, shows that the hope and confidence of pious men of old was in the Lord as their Rock, saying: "I will publish the name of the Lord: ascribe ye greatness unto our God. He is the Rock, His work is perfect: for all His ways are judgment: a God of truth and without iniquity, just and right is He." [Deut. 32:3, 4] The saintly Hannah, rejoicing over her relief from deep distress, clearly stated that God was the rock upon which she anchored her soul. She said: "There is none holy as the Lord: for there is none beside Thee: neither is there any rock like our God." [1 Sam 2:2] And David, who was the royal ancestor of Christ, uttered the following irrefutable and inspired testimony: "The Lord is my rock, and my fortress, and my deliverer; the God of my rock; in Him will I trust: He is my shield, and the horn of my salvation, my high tower, and my refuge, my Saviour; thou savest me from violence....For who is God, save the Lord? And who is a rock, save our God?" [2 Sam. 22:2, 3, 32]

According to the foregoing testimonies, it is an established fact that the doctrine of primacy of a human being as the foundation of the church of God was not admitted during the centuries before the birth of Christ.

Did Peter understand that Christ's words made him the rock upon which the Christian church is founded? Let Peter's own writings answer the question: "Wherefore also it is contained in the Scripture, Behold, I lay in Sion a chief corner stone, elect, precious: and he that believeth on Him shall not be confounded. Unto you therefore which

Peter and the Rock

believe He is precious: but unto them which be disobedient, the stone which the builders disallowed, the same is made the head of the corner, and a stone of stumbling, and a rock of offense, even to them which stumble at the word, being disobedient: whereunto also they were appointed." [1 Pet. 2:6–8; Isa. 28:16; Ps. 118:22, 23] Peter did not say, "He that believeth on me shall not be confounded." No, he said, "He that believeth on Him [that is, on Christ] shall not be confounded." The apostle was quoting a prophecy concerning Christ, one which the Master applied to Himself [Luke 20:16–18] and which Peter applied to Him, saying: "Be It known unto you all, and to all the people of Israel, that by the name of Jesus Christ of Nazareth, whom ye crucified, whom God raised from the dead, even by Him doth this man stand here before you whole. This is the stone which was set at nought by the builders, which is become the head of the corner. Neither is there salvation in any other: for there is none other name under heaven given among men, whereby we must be saved." [Acts 4:10–12] He further states in these texts that those who are disobedient reject Christ as the chief Rock.

The great apostle Paul, who classed himself a "wise masterbuilder," adds his testimony to that of Peter and gives Christ His rightful place as the foundation of the Christian religion: "According to the grace of God which is given unto me, as a wise masterbuilder, I have laid the foundation, and another buildeth thereon. But let every man take heed how he buildeth thereupon. For other foundation can no man lay than that is laid, which is Jesus Christ." [1 Cor. 3:10, 11] Again he clearly states that Christ was the Great Petra, or Rock, of "the church in the wilderness." [Acts 7:38] He said the Israelites "did all drink the same spiritual drink: for they drank of that spiritual Rock [*petra*] that followed them: and that Rock [*petra*] was Christ." [1 Cor. 10:4] "The Rock, the sure foundation upon which the church is built, is Jesus Christ.

The Wine of Roman Babylon

"Now therefore ye are no more strangers and foreigners, but fellowcitizens with the saints, and of the household of God; and are built upon the foundation of the apostles and prophets, 'Jesus Christ Himself being the Chief Cornerstone; in whom all the building fitly framed together groweth unto an holy temple in the Lord: in whom ye also are builded together for an habitation of God through the Spirit." [Eph. 2:19-22] Thus "the apostles and prophets" are given. equal honor, and no special distinction is given to Peter over the rest, in the foundation of the church, but the greatest honor belongs to Jesus Christ Himself, who is "the Chief Cornerstone," for it is He "in whom the building is made secure."

The Lord gives instruction for every man to take heed how he builds, and also that each one note what he builds upon. We are nearing the end of this world's history, and we need a firm foundation to give stability and security to our faith. This place of safety can be found only in Christ. When the storm breaks, those who are building upon the human will witness their structure crumbling in irretrievable ruin. It is our privilege to have the experience so beautifully expressed by Edward Mote in these words:

> "My hope is built on nothing less
> Than Jesus' blood and righteousness;
> I dare not trust the sweetest frame,
> But wholly lean on Jesus' name.
>
> "On Christ, the solid Rock, I stand;
> All other ground is sinking sand,
> All other ground is sinking sand."[67]

The Lord longs for the words so beautifully expressed in this hymn to be a living transaction in the lives of all who profess to be His followers. The great fountain of the Written Word is open to all, and the satisfactoriness of that

---
67   Edward Mote, hymn "My Hope Is Built on Nothing Less."

life-giving stream will more than compensate for any adjustment that one may have to make in his religious belief in order to conform to God's will.

Also see Appendix p. 211.

This view of the colorful Easter service in St. Peter's in Rome shows the Roman Pontiff, Pius XII, sitting on his throne immediately after delivering a message on world peace. The Roman pope claims to be the viceregent of God on earth and the absolute ruler over the Christian church. (Photo by Wide World.)

CHAPTER X

Peter and the Keys

THE NINTH sip of Babylon's wine may be entitled "Peter and the Keys." The doctrine of the Petrine primacy is alleged to be based on the following statement made by Christ: "And I will give unto thee the keys of the kingdom of heaven: and whatsoever thou shalt bind on earth shall be bound in heaven: and whatsoever thou shalt loose on earth shall be loosed in heaven." [Matt. 16:19, 20]

What are these keys that are so effective in the opening and the closing of the kingdom of heaven? The keys which Jesus entrusted to His disciples are His own words, which include both the Old and the New Testament., It is the Holy Bible that has the power to open and shut heaven. "These have power to shut heaven, that it rain not in the days of their prophecy: and have power over waters to turn them to blood, and to smite the earth with all plagues, as often as they will." [Rev. 11:6]

The Old Testament writings had declared the Christ of prophecy. Another set of sacred writings which would bear witness to the fulfillment of prophecy in the life, death, burial, and resurrection of Christ, was to be penned by divine inspiration. This collection known as the New Testament, reveals Jesus Christ as the head of the church, the cornerstone of the spiritual structure, and the sure foundation of the church of God. The New Testament Scriptures are they that record the glorious ascension of the Son of God to heaven and His inauguration as our great

High Priest in the sanctuary above. Furthermore, they reveal more fully that the hope of the Christian down through the ages will be completely realized at the second coming of Jesus Christ. This glorious hope is one of the main themes of the New Testament. These two keys to the heavenly kingdom, which are the Old and the New Testament, Christ entrusted to Peter and the other disciples, and they constitute a complete guidebook of instruction to His church.

The Holy Scriptures alone are the infallible guidebook and declare the conditions upon which men are received or denied entrance into the kingdom of heaven. The right use of these keys, which is the proper preaching of the word of God, opens the door of eternal life to the one who is willing to obey God, but it closes the door to all who refuse to obey Him. The gospel ministry is the most glorious work ever committed to men. It carries with it a very grave responsibility, for every gospel worker is either a savor of life unto life or of death unto death. The sacred keys, rightfully used, will not only open heaven to human hearts but will instruct them in the way of eternal life.

God used Peter, after his conversion, to employ the keys—the Sacred Scriptures—to unlock the kingdom of heaven to hearts that heretofore had not accepted Christ. The secret of Peter's success on the day of Pentecost, when 3,000 souls were converted, was his use of the Divine Word. The Old Testament Scriptures were the basis of his teachings, as the opening words of his address clearly show: "But this is that which was spoken by the prophet Joel." [Acts 2:16, 17; Joel 2:28] Throughout his wonderful discourse he shows his familiarity with the Old Testament, particularly the prophecies relating to the Messiah.

The teaching of the word of God by Peter to Cornelius and his household opened the kingdom of heaven to them. [Acts 10]

The great apostle Paul, in his mission travels, found the doors of heathen fields and pagan hearts thrown open to him. Note his words: "A great door and effectual is opened unto me." [1 Cor. 16:9] His testimony of his strict adherence to the Written Word in all his preaching is expressed in the following statement: "Having therefore obtained help of God, I continue unto this day, witnessing both to small and great, saying none other things than those which the prophets and Moses did say should come." [Acts 26:22] "But this I confess unto thee, that after the way which they call heresy, so worship I the God of my fathers, believing all things which are written in the law and in the prophets." [Acts 24:14]

When Timothy was charged by Paul to make good use of the keys by faithful preaching, he added that the time would come when fables would be preferred in place of God's word: "I charge thee therefore before God, and the Lord Jesus Christ, who shall judge the quick and the dead at His appearing and His kingdom; preach the word; be instant in season, out of season; reprove, rebuke, exhort with all longsuffering and doctrine. For the time will come when they will not endure sound doctrine; but after their own lusts shall they heap to themselves teachers, having itching ears; and they shall turn away their ears from the truth, and shall be turned unto fables." [2 Tim. 4:1-4] This admonition which the veteran apostle gave to that youthful preacher ought to be heeded by all clergymen, both Roman Catholic and Protestant.

Although keys are instruments which open and shut doors, the way in which they are used is of vital importance. By false preaching the doctrines of the Holy Scriptures may be wrested [2 Pet. 3:16] from their true meaning. In the days of Christ certain religious leaders had the keys, but instead of using them to open the kingdom of heaven, they locked it so their followers could not enter. Their wrong course was denounced by the Son of God, who said

The Wine of Roman Babylon

to them: "But woe unto you, scribes and Pharisees, hypocrites! For ye shut up the kingdom of heaven against men: for ye neither go in yourselves, neither suffer ye them that are entering to go in....Woe unto you, scribes and Pharisees, hypocrites! For ye compass sea and land to make one proselyte, and when he is made, ye make him twofold more the child of hell than yourselves." [Matt. 23:13, 15]

The exaltation of human tradition above the word of God has wrought detriment to Christianity and has resulted in the loss of souls. Christ said to religious teachers of His day: "Thus have ye made the commandment of God of none effect by your tradition. Ye hypocrites, well did Esaias prophesy of you, saying, This people draweth nigh unto Me with their mouth, and honoreth Me with their lips; but their heart is far from Me. But in vain they do worship Me, teaching for doctrines the commandments of men....Let them alone: they be blind leaders of the blind. And if the blind lead the blind, both shall fall into the ditch." [Matt. 15:6-9, 14]

God's warning against tampering with His written revelation has not been withdrawn, and those today who presume to teach doctrines of men in place of those of the Holy Bible will find some day that they have forfeited their hope of eternal life, and have destroyed the hope of those who have followed their example and teaching. To take away or withhold the key that opens to men the knowledge of Christ is a solemn thing, and a woe is pronounced upon those who are guilty: "Woe unto you, lawyers! For ye have taken away the key of knowledge: ye entered not in yourselves, and them that were entering in ye hindered." [Luke 11:52]

Though all Christian ministers are given the power to use the keys—the Holy Scriptures—to open the kingdom of heaven to the hearts of their hearers, the exclusive right to admit or to debar an individual from heaven is the prerogative of Christ alone. The experience of Jesus with James and John in the matter of dealing with the Samaritans, who differed with them on points of religion, bears out the truth that such ower, if invested in men, would be dangerous. "[He] sent messengers before His face: and they went, and entered into a village of the Samaritans, to make ready for Him. And they did not receive Him, because His face was as though He would go to Jerusalem. And when His disciples James and John saw this, they said, Lord, wilt Thou that we command fire to come down from heaven, and consume them, even as Elias did? But He turned, and rebuked them, and said, Ye know not what manner of spirit ye are of ." [Luke 9:52-55]

History tells a long, sad story of religious persecutions, and the shores of time are strewn with the victims of religious bigotry. Our all-wise God, knowing that the heart of man would not be magnanimous enough in dealing with those who should differ from him, put the key to the portals of heaven beyond his reach. That key He keeps in His own hand. "And to the angel of the church in Philadelphia write: These things saith He that is holy, He that is true, He that hath the key of David, He that openeth, and no man shutteth; and shutteth, and no man openeth." [Rev. 3:7]

If Peter had been invested with pontifical authority by Christ, why did he not occupy the chair and preside over the first great church council, which was held at Jerusalem? It was James who presided, and he announced the decision made there. "And after they had held their peace, James answered, saying, Men and brethren, hearken unto me: Wherefore my sentence is, that we trouble not them, which from among the Gentiles are turned to God: but that we write unto them," etc. [Acts 15:13, 19, 20] James's final word, which sealed the deliberation of this council, is sufficient proof that Peter was not recognized then by the apostolic church or by the other apostles as being supreme. Peter doubtless would have displayed his pontifical power in this council if he had been invested with such; but the Sacred Record says absolutely nothing to indicate that the primacy belonged to Peter.

If the Roman Catholic Church's claims are true that Peter held the supreme episcopal power, is it not strange that Paul was not informed about it? Paul publicly rebuked Peter at Antioch. Paul said:

"But when Peter was come to Antioch, I withstood him to the face, because he was to be blamed. For before that certain came from James, he did eat with the Gentiles: but when they were come, he withdrew and separated himself, fearing them which were of the circumcision. And the other Jews dissembled likewise with him; insomuch that Barnabas also was carried away with their dissimulation. But when I saw that they walked not uprightly according to the truth of the gospel, I said unto Peter before them all, If thou, being a Jew, livest after the manner of Gentiles, and not as do the Jews, why compellest thou the Gentiles to live as do the Jews?" [Gal. 2:11-14]

However, Paul did pay tribute to religious authority when it was due, for he apologized to Ananias upon discovering that he had not recognized the high priest's sacred office: "And Paul, earnestly beholding the council, said, Men and brethren, I have lived in all good conscience before God until this day. And the high priest Ananias commanded them that stood by him to smite him on the mouth. Then said Paul unto him, God shall smite thee, thou whited wall: for sittest thou to judge me after the law, and commandest me to be smitten contrary to the law? And they that stood by said, Revilest thou God's high priest? Then said Paul, I wist not, brethren, that he was the high priest: for it is written, Thou shalt not speak evil of the ruler of thy people." [Acts 23:1-5]

When Paul made the statement, "I suppose I was not a whit behind the very chiefest apostles," [2 Cor. 11:5] he evidently recognized more than one person as having the supreme authority in the church, as the plural word "apostles" indicates. He put himself on a par with the chiefest of the leaders of the church, thus showing that all were on equality in its leadership.

If a pontifical office had been established by Christ, with Peter occupying it, neither Paul nor the rest of the apostles would ever have assumed the attitude they did in matters of directing the church.

Did the apostle Peter himself believe that Jesus had made him the head of His church, and that He had given him ecclesiastical authority to dictate to other men what they should believe and do? Peter's attitude toward the honor paid him by Cornelius shows that he rejected such homage as is paid to the bishop of Rome today. "And as Peter was coming in, Cornelius met him, and fell down at his feet, and worshiped him. But Peter took him up, saying, Stand up; I myself also am a man." [Acts 10:25, 26]

Instead of making an assumptive claim of being lord over the flock, Peter declared himself to be on equality with the other ministers and denounced any who might have the tendency toward exactions in any form. He recognized only Christ as the Chief Shepherd, or head, of the church. "The elders which are among you I exhort, who am also an elder, and a witness of the sufferings of Christ, and also a partaker of the glory that shall be revealed: feed the flock of God which is among you, taking the oversight thereof, not by constraint, but willingly; not for filthy lucre, but of a ready mind; neither as being lords over God's heritage, but being ensamples to the flock. And when the Chief Shepherd shall appear, ye shall receive a crown of glory that fadeth not away." [1 Pet. 5:1–4]

The Wine of Roman Babylon

Peter loved his Lord, and throughout his Christian life he maintained a humble spirit. Affluence, pride, social standing, regal power, and supreme authority over his colaborers in the gospel ministry were foreign to the unobtrusive Peter.

Christ warned His disciples against singling out one man to be the head of His flock, saying to them: "But be not ye called Rabbi: for one is your Master, even Christ; and all ye are brethren. And call no man your father upon the earth for one is your Father, which is in heaven. Neither be ye. called masters: for one is your Master, even Christ." [Matt. 23:8-10]

The Mighty Rock, Christ Jesus, is our only infallible guide; and, thank God, He is the head over all things in the church. "The head of every man is Christ."[1 Cor. 11:3] God "hath put all things under His feet, and gave Him to be the head over all things to the church, which is His body, the fullness of Him that filleth all in all." [Eph. 1:22, 23]

After examining this array of evidence from the Sacred Book, and seeing that Christ is the head and the foundation of His church, how can any one hold to the doctrine of the primacy of Peter and admit the supposedly apostolic succession alleged by the popes of Rome? Here is the reasoning set forth by two papal writers:

> "If the proprietor of a house, on leaving it for the summer, says to any friend: 'Here are the keys of my house,' would not this simple declaration, without a word of explanation, convey the idea, 'I give you full control of my house; you may admit or exclude whom you please; you represent me in my absence'? Let us now apply this interpretation to our Redeemer's words. When He says to Peter:' I will give to thee the keys,' etc., He evidently means: I will give the supreme authority over My church, which is the citadel of faith, My earthly Jerusalem. Thou and thy successors shall be My visible representatives to the end of time.'"[68]

---

[68] Gibbons, 100, 101.

Peter and the Keys

"The primacy of St. Peter and the perpetuity of that primacy in the Roman see are dogmatically defined in the canons attached to the first two chapters of the constitution 'Pastor Æternus': (a) 'If anyone shall say that blessed Peter the apostle was not constituted by Christ our Lord as chief of all the apostles and the visible head of the whole church militant; or that he did not receive directly and immediately from the same Lord Jesus Christ a primacy of true and proper jurisdiction, but one of honor only: let him be anathema.' (b) 'If any one shall say that it is not by the institution of Christ our Lord Himself or by divinely established right that blessed Peter has perpetual successors in his primacy over the universal church: or that the Roman pontiff is not the successor of blessed Peter in this same primacy:—let him be anathema.'"[69]

The imbibing of this false doctrine has resulted in the exaltation of the "man of sin" to his elevated position, thus fulfilling the prophecy made by the apostle Paul centuries ago, when he said: "Let no man deceive you by any means: for that day shall not come, except there come a falling away first, and that man of sin be revealed, the son of perdition; who opposeth and exalteth himself above all that is called God, or that is worshiped; so that be as God sitteth in the temple of God, showing himself that he is God." [2 Thess. 2:3, 4]

To whom did the prophetic utterance of Paul refer? It can apply only to the head of the Roman Catholic Church. This their own works disclose. We read:

"While the [Roman] Church lasts, Peter (and his successors) will hold its keys. Christ, who has the 'key of the house of David,' Christ, who opens and no man shuts, shuts and no man opens, continues to be the Master of the house; but Peter is the steward to whom the keys are committed. He admits to and excludes from the church in his Master's name. In other words, he is the center of the church's unity. All, from the great apostle of the Gentiles down to the most obscure of the

---

[69] "Pope," *The Catholic Encyclopedia* v12, 265.

church's children, hold their place and exercise their functions in subordination to Peter....

"What he binds and looses on earth is bound and loosed in heaven, i.e., he is the ultimate earthly judge of what is lawful and unlawful. He is to lay down the laws and conditions on which communion with the church and participation in its privileges depend, and the decisions of his tribunal here will be ratified hi the heavenly court."[70]

The authority to discipline or to excommunicate a church member was never entrusted to one individual. It was given to the church as a whole. The Lord has given this great power not to any one man but to His church as a body. The procedure to be followed in matters of disciplining her members is explicitly laid down by Him in the Sacred Word:

"Moreover if thy brother shall trespass against thee, go and tell him his fault between thee and him alone: if he shall hear thee, thou hast gained thy brother. But if he will not hear thee, then take with thee one or two more, that in the mouth of two or three witnesses every word may be established. And if he shall neglect to hear them, tell it unto the church: but if he neglect to hear the church, let him be unto thee as an heathen man and a publican. Verily I say unto you, Whatsoever ye shall bind on earth shall be bound in heaven: and whatsoever ye shall loose on earth shall be loosed in heaven." [Matt. 18:15–18]

If the course which the Lord prescribes is faithfully followed, then whatsoever *the church* binds on earth will be bound in heaven. God ratifies her decision when she follows the instructions He has laid down in the Bible. The Lord has never given license to any one individual of the church to sit in judgment on the sins of others, nor to dictate to the believers in matters of doctrine. The highest authority is invested in the church as a body. But the claims

---

[70] Wm. E. Addis and Thomas Arnold, "Pope," *A Catholic Dictionary*, 669.

Peter and the Keys

of the Roman Church about the primacy of Peter are extravagant:

> "Further, Peter's authority is subordinated to no earthly superior. The sentences which he gives are to be forthwith ratified in heaven. They do not need the antecedent approval of any other tribunal. He is independent of all save the Master who appointed him. The words as to the power of binding and loosing are, therefore, elucidatory of the promise of the keys which immediately precedes. They explain in what sense Peter is governor and head of Christ's kingdom, the church, by promising him legislative and judicial authority in the fullest sense. In other words, Peter and his successors have power to impose laws both preceptive and prohibitive, power likewise to grant dispensation from these laws, and, when needful, to annul them. It is theirs to judge offences against the laws, to impose and to remit penalties. This judicial authority will even include the power to pardon sin. For sin is a breach of the laws of the supernatural kingdom, and falls under the cognizance of its constituted judges."[71]

Contrary to the instruction contained in the Bible, the bishop of Rome assumes the supreme right to bind, to loose, to legislate, to convoke, to abrogate, to interpret, to beatify, to canonize, to excommunicate and to hurl anathemas against the mightiest of earthly potentates as well as against the humblest of his subjects. Here are some of the prerogatives which are said to belong to him:

> "(1) As the supreme teacher of the church, whose it is to prescribe what is to be believed by all the faithful, and to take measures for the preservation and the propagation of the faith, the following are the rights which pertain to the pope: (a) it is his to set forth creeds, and to determine when and by whom an explicit profession of faith shall be made (cf. Council of Trent, Sess. XXIV, cc.i,xii); (b) it is his to prescribe and to command books for the religious instruction of the faithful; thus, for example, Clement XIII has recommended the Roman Catechism to all the bishops. (c) The pope alone

---

[71] "Pope," *The Catholic Encyclopedia* v12, 265.

can establish a university, possessing the status and privileges of a canonically erected [Roman] Catholic university; (d) to him also belongs the direction of [Roman] Catholic missions throughout the world; this charge is fulfilled through the Congregation of the Propaganda. (e) It is his to prohibit the reading of such books as are injurious to faith or morals, and to determine the conditions on which certain classes of books may be issued by (Roman] Catholics; (f) his is the condemnation of given propositions as being either heretical or deserving of some minor degree of censure, and lastly (g) he has the right to interpret authentically the natural law. Thus, it is his to say what is lawful or unlawful in regard to social and family life, in regard to the practice of usury, etc.

"With the pope's office of supreme teacher are closely connected his rights in regard to the worship of God: for it is the law of prayer that fixes the law of belief. In this sphere very much has been reserved to the sole regulation of the Holy See. Thus (a) the pope alone can prescribe the liturgical services employed in the [Roman] Church. If a doubt should occur in regard to the ceremonial of the liturgy, a bishop may not settle the point on his own authority, but must have recourse to Rome. The Holy See likewise prescribes rules in regard to the devotions used by the faithful, and in this way checks the growth of what is novel and unauthorized. (b) At the present day the institution and abrogation of festivals, which was till a comparatively recent time free to all bishops as regards their own dioceses, is reserved to Rome. (c) The solemn canonization of a saint is proper to the pope. Indeed it is commonly held that this is an exercise of the papal infallibility. Beatification and every permission for the public veneration of any of the servants of God is likewise reserved to his decision. (d) He alone gives to anyone the privilege of a private chapel where mass may be said. (e) He dispenses the treasury of the [Roman] Church, and the grant of plenary indulgences is reserved to him. While he has no authority in regard to the substantial rites of the sacraments, and is bound to reserve them as they were given to the church by Christ and His apostles, certain powers in their regard belong to him; (f) he can give to simple priests the power to confirm, and to bless the oil of the sick and the oil of catechumens, and (g) he can establish diriment and impedient impediments to matrimony.

"(3) The legislative power of the pope carries with it the following rights: (a) he can legislate for the whole church, with or without the assistance of a general council; (b) if he legislates with the aid of a council, it is his to convoke it, to preside, to direct its deliberations, to confirm its acts. (c) He has full authority to interpret, alter, and abrogate both his own laws and those established by his predecessors. He has the same plentitude of power as they enjoyed, and stands in the same relation to their laws as to those which he himself has decreed; (d) he can dispense individuals from the obligation of all purely ecclesiastical laws, and can grant privileges and exemptions in their regard. In this connection may be mentioned (e) his power to dispense from vows where the greater glory of God renders it desirable. Considerable powers of dispensation are granted to bishops, and, in a restricted measure, also to priests; but there are some vows reserved altogether to the Holy See.[72]

It is by usurpation that the Roman pope assumes the power that he claims. Christ has never bestowed this power upon him or any other individual. Such extraordinary power, such assumption of supremacy, as the pope claims to have, is clearly opposed to the teachings of the Sacred Scriptures. Those who acknowledge and implicitly obey the requirements of the papal head as an infallible guide, are elevating human laws and tradition above the expressed commands of God. "Thus saith the Lord: Cursed be the man that trusteth in man, and maketh flesh his arm, and whose heart departeth from the Lord.... Blessed is the man that trusteth in the Lord, and whose hope the Lord is." [Jer. 17:5, 7]

The man who styles himself the vicar of Christ is displaying the traits of character that actuated Lucifer, who said: "I will ascend into heaven, I will exalt my throne

---
[72] Ibid., 269.

above the stars of God: I will sit also upon the mount of the congregation, in the sides of the north: I will ascend above the heights of the clouds; I will be like the Most High." [Isa. 14:13, 14] Compare with this the claims made for the bishop of Rome:

"Q. Who is the holy father or pope? A. The holy father or pope is the visible head of the church, the successor of St. Peter and the vicar of Christ on earth."[73]

The Lord has left His vicar on earth to direct His church, but this vicegerent is the Holy Spirit. Christ said to the apostles: "But the Comforter, which is the Holy Ghost, whom the Father will send in My name, He shall teach you all things, and bring all things to your remembrance, whatsoever I have said unto you." [John 14:26] The Holy Spirit is the great teacher of the church.

Truly our God is long suffering, for He has borne all these centuries with a power that has usurped the prerogatives and office of Christ's vicar!

The Roman pope claims to be the successor of Peter. There is a vast difference between claiming the apostolic succession and possessing the apostolic attributes. This bold claim calls for the evidence of the life, character, and power of not only Peter but Jesus Himself. The pope is the antipode of Christ and Peter instead of their successor, just as the mystery of iniquity is the opposite of the mystery of godliness.

The Divine Word reveals that in Christ was the mystery of godliness, because of His coming to this earth to live a life of privation and suffer a shameful death. "And without controversy great is the mystery of godliness: God was manifest in the flesh, justified in the Spirit, seen of angels, preached unto the Gentiles, believed on in the world, received up into glory." [1 Tim. 3:16] Here is brought to

---

[73] P. Geiermann, *The Convert's Catechism of Catholic Doctrine* (1930, reprint, Brushton, New York: TEACH Services, Inc., 1995) 26.

view the wonderful condescension of the Son of God when He divested Himself of His glory and took upon Himself the form of sinful humanity. We have portrayed by the apostle Paul the sevenfold self-humiliation of Christ in the following words: "Let this mind be in you, which was also in Christ Jesus: who, being in the form of God, thought it not robbery to be equal with God: but made Himself of no reputation, and took upon Him the form of a servant, and was made in, the likeness of men: and being found in fashion as a man, He humbled Himself, and became obedient unto death, even the death of the cross." [Phil. 2:5-8]

The study of these verses enables us to comprehend more fully the mystery of godliness as seen in the wonderful condescension of Jesus Christ. Note the sevenfold steps which led to His complete humiliation:

1. *He emptied Himself of His glory.* "He divested Himself of the glories of heaven," says John Lightfoot.[74]

2. *He took the form of a servant.* To the natural heart nothing is more degrading than to become a servant, yet Christ was a servant of servants.

3. *He was made in the likeness of men.* He could not have sunk any lower in the scale of morally responsible beings than to be made in the likeness of sinful men, and partake of human nature with all its marks of degeneracy. Yet, He, the God of the universe, laid aside His glory and became a man.

4. *He was found in fashion as a man.* He was a common man. He had no social standing, no prestige, or influence, particularly none with the rich, or the aristocracy of His day. "He hath no form nor comeliness; and when we shall see Him, there is no beauty that we should desire Him. He is despised and rejected of men; a man of sorrows, and acquainted with grief: and we hid as it were our faces from

---

[74] J. B. Lightfoot, *Saint Paul's Epistle to the Philippians*, rev. text (New York: Macmillan & Company, 1894) 110.

Him; He was despised, and we esteemed Him not." [Isa. 53:2, 3] As a carpenter until He was thirty years of age, He had to share the lot of humanity under the curse of sin and earn His bread by the sweat of His brow. After entering upon His ministry, many times He slept under the canopy of heaven, partaking of the extreme hardships to which men are sometimes exposed. Those who are deprived of the bare necessities of life, such as food, drink, and the protection and comfort of a home, may find consolation in the fact that Jesus Christ Himself also experienced this lot of life, for it was a part of the bitterness of that cup which He drained for us. He said: "Foxes have holes, and birds of the air have nests; but the Son of man hath not where to lay His head." [Luke 9:58]

5. *He humbled Himself.* Christ was neither proud nor self-assertive. Though He was conscious of the fact that He was the God of the universe, He maintained His unpretentious and unassuming character throughout His life's journey. He was assailed repeatedly by arrogant priests on the question of His divinity, yet never once did He meet the challenge by displaying His power to bring glory to Himself. The humility which characterized His everyday life was paramount on all occasions, whether before a haughty ruler or before a commoner.

6. *He was obedient unto death.* Life is precious to all, as Satan's statement concerning Job indicates: "Yea, all that a man hath will he give for his life." [Job 2:4] Despite this truism, Christ demonstrated His divine love for those whom He came to save. Such love that actuated Him in dying for His enemies is beyond our capacity to understand.

7. *He suffered even the death of the cross.* Death on the tree was something disgraceful, dishonorable, and ignominious in Old Testament times. "And if a man have committed a sin worthy of death, and he be to be put to death, and

thou hang him on a tree: his body shall not remain all night upon the tree, but thou shalt in any wise bury him that day; (for he that is hanged is accursed of God)." [Deut. 21:22, 23]

Try to visualize the scene on Golgotha. Behold the Son of God hanging between heaven and earth, nailed on a shameful cross, and dying because His great heart of love prompted Him to pay the penalty for man. Ought it not to lead us to join in the. hymn of praise by Isaac Watts? Note his words:

> "When I survey the wondrous cross
> On which the Prince of glory died,
> My richest gain I count but loss,
> And pour contempt on all my pride.
>
> "See, from His head, His hands, His feet,
> Sorrow and love flow mingled down;
> Did e'er such love and sorrow meet?
> Or thorns compose so rich a crown?
>
> "Since I, who was undone and lost,
> Have pardon through His name and word;
> Forbid it, then, that I should boast,
> Save in the cross of Christ, my Lord."[75]

In Paul's definition of the "mystery of iniquity," he makes very clear what the steps were that led up to the development of the "man of sin." He said: "Let no man deceive you by any means: for that day shall not come, except there come a failing away first, and that man of sin be revealed, the son of perdition; who opposeth and exalteth himself above all that is called God, or that is worshiped; so that he as God sitteth in the temple of God, showing himself that he is God." [2 Thess. 2:3, 4, 7]

In contrast to the pure, humble, and self-sacrificing life of Christ, we see the proud, arrogant, and selfasserting pontiff. Behold his great claims:

---

[75] Isaac Watts, hymn "When I Survey the Wondrous Cross."

The Wine of Roman Babylon

"The pope is the vicar of Christ, or the visible head of the church on earth. The claims of the pope are the same as the claims of Christ. Christ wanted all souls saved. So does the pope. Christ can forgive all sin. So can the pope. The pope is the only man who claims the vicarage of Christ. His claim is not seriously opposed, and this establishes his authority."[76]

And Leo XIII, speaking for the Roman bishops, said: "We hold upon this earth the place of God Almighty."[77]

Let us take the words which portray the condescension of Christ and contrast them with statements used to describe the man who aspires to be God. Without controversy, great is the mystery of iniquity! Seven steps which led to the self-exaltation of the "man of sin" are as follows:

1. *Emptied himself of humanity.* It has been said of the pope: "Thou art the shepherd, thou art the physician, thou art the director, thou art the husbandman; finally, thou art another God on earth."[78] Emptying himself of the status of a common man, the Roman bishop clothed himself with the prerogatives of divinity, assuming titles and powers that belong to the Deity alone.

2. *He assumed the form of a lord instead of a servant.* To the unregenerated heart, nothing is more natural than to manifest the spirit of a master. This the pope has done, when he assumed jurisdiction not only over the people on this earth but also over heavenly angels as well. One papal authority says: "Moreover the superiority and the power of the Roman pontiff by no means pertain only to heavenly

---

[76] Extract from a sermon preached by Jeremiah Prendergast, S. J., in the Church of St. John the Baptist, in Syracuse, New York, on Wednesday evening, March 13, 1912. (Reported in the Syracuse *Post-Standard*, March 14. 1912).

[77] Leo XIII, in the encyclical letter, *The Reunion of Christendom*, dated June 20, 1894. See *The Great Encyclical Letters of Leo XIII*, 3rd edition, 304.

[78] An extract from the oration delivered by Christopher Marcellus in the fourth session of the Fifth Lateran Council (1512), when addressing the Roman pope. See P. Labbe and g. Cossart, *Sacrosancta Concilia*, v14, col. 109.

things, to earthly things, and to things under the earth, but are even over angels, than whom he is greater."[79]

3. *He made himself an alter Christus ("another Christ")*. We read again: "The pope is of so great dignity and so exalted that he is not a mere man, but as it were God, and the vicar of God."[80] No greater self-exaltation could be assumed by a man.

4. *He is found in fashion as the vicar of God.* "The pope is as it were God on earth, sole sovereign of the faithful of Christ, chief king of kings, having plenitude of power, to whom has been intrusted by the omnipotent God direction not only of the earthly but also of the heavenly kingdom."[81] He has not only ecclesiastical power but also social and political standing coupled with the display of worldly possessions, pomp, dignity of office, scholarship, and prestige. All of this is contrary to the spirit and life of the meek and lowly Jesus who had not where to lay His head, and of the penniless Peter who did not have a coin to give to the beggar who sat at the gate of the temple." [Acts 3:6]

5. *He exalted himself.* Here is the claim made for the bishop of Rome: "The pope is of such lofty and supreme dignity that, properly speaking, he has not been established in any rank of dignity, but rather has been placed upon the very summit of all ranks of dignities.

"The pope is called most holy because he is rightfully presumed to be such."

"He is likewise the divine monarch and supreme emperor, and king of kings."

"Hence the pope is crowned with a triple crown, as king of heaven and of earth and of the lower regions."[82]

---

[79] Lucius Ferraris,"Papa," *Prompta Bibliotheca* v6 (Venice, Italy: Gaspar Storti, 1772) 26–41. *The Catholic Encyclopedia* ("Ferraris," v6, 48) speaks of this ecclesiastical dictionary as "a precious mine of information."
[80] Ibid.
[81] Ibid.
[82] Ibid.

The Wine of Roman Babylon

He is both proud and assertive, and his exalted claims make him both pretentious and assuming in character. This spirit of exaltation is foreign to the life of Christ.

6. *Whereas Christ became obedient unto death, the Roman pope lives in ease and luxury.* Christ's power of love was demonstrated by His death on the cross, while the exalted man on the papal throne displays his love for power. The bishop of Rome dwells in a palatial atmosphere of protection, and everything that belongs to a life of luxury is his. Surrounded by the Swiss guard and the pomp of the Vatican, he holds nothing in common with the unguarded Christ whose representative he claims to be.

7. *There is nothing shameful about the death of a bishop of Rome.* Compare the worldly display evidenced at the demise of a Roman pope with that of the humble Galilean's death. The penury of the Son of God would have caused Him to be buried in a pauper's grave, if it had not been for the kindness of Joseph of Arimathea. The esteem with which the papal head is held by the potentates of earth, and the veneration shown to him by his own subjects, make his death and burial a striking contrast to Christ's martyrdom.

One day I stood in the Piazza S. Pietro in Rome and viewed the so-called Basilica of St. Peter. Gazing upon this beautiful edifice, whose cornerstone was laid by Julius II in 1506, I was convinced that more grandeur is probably displayed in and about this temple than can be found anywhere else on earth. It doubtless has no rival. The vastness of St. Peter's Square with its proud colonnades, the Egyptian obelisk with the cross placed upon it, towering into the heavens, the sparkling fountains that radiate the colors of the rainbow when light is focused upon them, the stately dome of the church so gorgeously illuminated, present a scene of indescribable glory, attract admirers, and subdue spectators. On entering the basilica, the beholder is met with extravagance and terrestrial glory on every hand.

Blended with all this display of worldly glory and seeming piety can be seen that which the word of God thunders against, the adoration and veneration of the deceased Peter. As I beheld men, women, and children from all walks and stations of life paying homage to the supposed image of Peter, each one bowing before it and touching its extended toe, this question arose in my mind: If the humble fisherman apostle were to come back to life and behold the place assigned to him in Roman Catholic worship, what would he think? Would not his indignation be aroused to repudiate such man-worship, as he did in the case of Cornelius of old. "And as Peter was coming in, Cornelius met him, and fell down at his feet, and worshiped him. But Peter took him up, saying, Stand up; I myself also am a man." [Acts 10:25, 26] His voice would be heard throughout the spacious basilica, saying: "We ought to obey God rather than men." [Acts 5:29] Also: "Neither is there salvation in any other: for there is none other name under heaven given among men, whereby we must be saved." [Acts 4:12]

The belief and acceptance of this papal doctrine—that our Lord entrusted the keys of the kingdom of heaven exclusively to Peter—has given rise to numerous arrogant assumptions by the bishops of Rome. The Roman Church claims that by some mysterious power the apostle's succession has been preserved and perpetuated by the occupants of the see of Rome. The superhuman power and unlimited authority which are ascribed to every Roman pope are beyond the comprehension of the average, non-Catholic. His pre-eminence and alleged infallibility extend beyond the ecclesiastical realm to the civil domain, and it is contended that his jurisdiction over both cannot be controverted because he is the possessor of the keys bestowed by our Lord upon Peter. The man who professes to hold such extraordinary and exclusive prerogatives must be intoxicated with a passion for power, praise, and opulence beyond the comprehension of the ordinary mind.

What a strange infatuation, when a people choose to pay homage to a human being exalted in place of their divine Creator and Redeemer! The message which God gives to the world today is: "Fear God, and give glory to Him." [Rev. 14:7] When this message is heeded, God is given His rightful place on the throne of the heart of the individual, and Christ is honored as the head of His church and the center of all its worship.

Also see the Appendix p. 213.

CHAPTER XI

The Immaculate Conception

THE TENTH sip from the cup of Babylon's wine, which we shall call "The Immaculate Conception," is one of profound importance. Mariolatry is practiced by every devout Roman Catholic. There are myriads of churches and altars erected to Mary all over the world, and all pay her homage. They bow at her shrine to worship and to pray to her as their mediatrix. In their prayers to her they give expression not only to an impoverished spiritual condition but also to an unbounded confidence in her as the great liberator of the oppressed soul, as the following words will attest:

"Remember, O most gracious virgin Mary, that never was it known that anyone who fled to thy protection, implored thy help, and sought thy intercession, was left unaided. Inspired with this confidence, I fly unto thee, O virgin of virgins, my mother. To thee I come, before thee I stand, sinful and sorrowful. O mother of the Word Incarnate, despise not my petitions, but in thy mercy hear and answer me. Amen."[83]

Another papal writer quotes this prayer:

"O Mary, we poor sinners know no other refuge than thee, for thou art our only hope, and on thee we rely for our salvation. Thou art our only advocate with Jesus Christ; to thee we all turn ourselves."[84]

---
[83] MacEachen, 15.
[84] Alfonsus M. de Liguori, *The Glories of Mary*, rev. by Robert A. Coffin, (London: Burns, Oates & Washbourne Ltd., 1868) 96.

The Wine of Roman Babylon

It is astonishing to find that centuries passed before the doctrine of the immaculate conception of Mary was accepted by the Roman Church as a dogma. The following statement taken from Cardinal Gibbons's works acknowledges that the "immaculate conception was not formulated into a dogma of faith till 1854....It is in strict harmony with the place which Mary holds in the economy of redemption."[85]

It was on December 8, 1854, that Pius IX, with 600 other bishops issued the famous bull that forever stilled a controversy which had existed among Roman Catholics for centuries.

"The bull *Ineffabilis* of Pius IX, December, 1854, declares 'that the doctrine which holds that the blessed virgin Mary, at the very first instance of her conception, by a singular grace and privilege of the Omnipotent God, in virtue of the merits of Jesus Christ, the Saviour of mankind, was preserved free from all stain of original sin, has been revealed by God, and therefore should firmly and constantly be believed by all the faithful.'"[86]

By the generality of Roman Catholics the date of December 8 is accepted as the feast of the Immaculate Conception without a word of remonstrance. Is it not strange that more people are not inclined to investigate the origin of the doctrines they hold? Such an investigation would lead them to acknowledge that the Roman Catholic Church's position on this subject is diametrically opposed to the teachings of the word of God. The papal church teaches that an immaculate mother had to be provided, alleging that Christ would not consent to become incarnate in flesh defiled by sin. Says one papal doctor:

"It was becoming that the Son should have an immaculate mother. He Himself chose Mary for His mother. It is impossible to believe that a son who could have a queen for his

---

[85] Gibbons, 171.
[86] Conway, 375.

The Immaculate Conception

mother would choose a slave. How, then, can we imagine that the Eternal Word, who could have an ever-immaculate mother, and one who had always been the friend of God, would have one defiled by sin, and at one time the enemy of God? Moreover, as an ancient author says, 'the flesh of Christ is the flesh of Mary.' The Son of God would have felt horror to have taken flesh of a Saint Agnes, a Saint Gertrude, or of a Saint Teresa, because these holy virgins were defiled by sin before baptism; and therefore the devil could then have reproached Him with being clothed with flesh which had once been subject to him. But as Mary was always pure and immaculate, our Lord felt no horror at becoming man in her chaste womb. Besides, Saint Thomas says, that 'Mary was preserved from every actual sin, even venial;' for otherwise she would not have been a becoming mother of God; but how much less would she have been so, had she been defiled by original sin, which renders the soul hateful to God?"[87]

Does the Written Word support the doctrine of the immaculate conception of Mary? Let Mary herself answer the question.: "And Mary said, My soul doth magnify the Lord, and my spirit hath rejoiced in God my Saviour." [Luke 1:46, 47] Mary said, "My Saviour," thus signifying that she needed a Redeemer, one who saves from sin.

Years after Mary was born, the apostle Paul, writing under divine inspiration, declared that "all have sinned, and come short of the glory of God." [Rom. 3:23] It is quite evident, therefore, that the Lord did not reveal to him the doctrine of the immaculate conception.

Such teaching strikes at the very heart of the gospel. If Mary was immaculately conceived, as the Roman Catholic Church claims, she would not have given Christ a body "in the likeness of sinful flesh," [Rom. 8:3] and He could not have been tempted as we are by Satan. The record of His life attests to the fact that Satan followed His steps indefatigably from the moment He was born until the time of His

---

[87] de Liguori, 643.

death. Why was the Son of God spending hours and nights in prayer to His heavenly Father for power to meet the enemy, if He were immune to sin? The apostle speaks of Him as one "who in the days of His flesh, when He had offered up prayers and supplications with strong crying and tears unto Him that was able to save Him from death, and was heard in that He feared; though He were a Son, yet learned He obedience by the things which He suffered; and being made perfect, He became the author of eternal salvation unto all them that obey Him." [Heb. 5:7-9]

All that Mary gave to Christ was His human body. It is a law of nature that one cannot give what one does not possess, and Mary, being human in every aspect of the word, could not impart to her Son the nature of, divinity. Christ's divine nature was from the days of eternity, even before the earth or Mary ever existed. [Mic. 5:2, margin; John 1:1-3, 10, 14; 17:5, 24; Col. 1:13-17; 1 Peter 1:19, 20] In His many experiences while here on earth, His dual nature (the human with the divine) stood out in marked contrast to each other. For instance, as a result of forty days of fasting in the wilderness "He was afterward an hungered." [Matt. 4:2] Yet He was the same being who exercised His divine power to miraculously feed thousands with a few loaves and fishes. [Luke 9:12-17] Again we see His human side when He was so weary that He fell asleep in the stem of the ship, while the disciples struggled helplessly with the boisterous sea. On being aroused by the words, "Master, carest Thou not that we perish?" Christ arose, lifted up His hand and displayed His divine power by rebuking the storm. [Mark 4:36-41] We have both the human and the divine of Christ manifested at Jacob's well, when He said to the woman of Samaria, "Give Me to drink," which showed that He was so human as to be suffering from physical thirst. And yet He was so divine that He could say to this same woman: "Whosoever drinketh of the water that I shall give him

The Immaculate Conception

shall never thirst; but the water that I shall give him shall be in him a well of water springing up into everlasting life." [John 4:7, 14]

In the biblical record of the experience of the arrest of Christ by the officers of the chief priest we have both His human and His divine natures again revealed. The human was noticeably evident when He permitted Himself to be taken by the officers of the law. In contrast to this, His divinity was exhibited by causing His captors to fall to the ground when He uttered the words, "I am He." [John 18:4–6]

If there were not another inspired statement dealing with this subject, the following one alone ought to settle forever in our minds the question of what kind of flesh it was in which Christ dwelt. "For what the law could not do, in that it was weak through the flesh, God sending His own Son in the likeness of sinful flesh, and for sin, condemned sin in the flesh." [Rom. 8:3]

There were reasons why Christ took upon Himself human flesh. The first was that He might demonstrate before the holy angels, the worlds on high, and Satan himself that it was possible for one, through the power given Him from God His Father, to live a life of perfect obedience to the commandments of God. "Forasmuch then as the children are partakers of flesh and blood, He also Himself likewise took part of the same; that through death He might destroy him that had the power of death, that is, the devil." [Heb. 2:14]

The second reason why He became bone of our bone and flesh of our flesh was that He might be able to sympathize with us poor sinful beings in our varied temptations and human weaknesses. "Wherefore in all things it behooved Him to be made like unto His brethren, that He might be a merciful and, faithful high priest in things pertaining to God, to make reconciliation for the sins of the people. For in that He Himself hath suffered being tempted, He is able to succor them that are tempted." [Heb. 2:17, 18] When we are tempted, it is a comfort to know that there is One who, having passed through like experiences, understands the power of the enemy and can give not only solace but strength to overcome the temptations. If it were true that Christ had been born of an immaculate mother, it would have rendered Him incapable of participating in our feelings when we are tempted and tried.

In the genealogy of Christ as given in Matthew we find Jesus called the Son of David and also the Son of Abraham. One has to study only the characters of Abraham and David to learn that they were very human and had a tendency to sin. Thus we see what kind of human nature Christ inherited from His progenitors.

If the doctrine of Mariolatry was to be promulgated through the ages, why is it that the Sacred Word records no divine instructions to that effect? If Mary was to be venerated and worshiped, is it not strange that Christ was silent in regard to it? However, there was another woman, Mary of Bethany, whose noble deed has inspired myriads through the ages to pour out their hearts' affections on their Saviour by means of gifts and sacrifices. This Mary's deed was immortalized by the statement of Christ when He said: "Verily I say unto you, Wheresoever this gospel shall be preached in the whole world, there shall also this, that this woman hath done, be told for a memorial of her." [Matt. 26:13]

Those who hold the doctrine of Mariolatry will be profoundly astonished when they analyze notable statements made by Christ concerning His mother. "While He yet talked to the people, behold, His mother and His brethren stood without, desiring to speak with Him. Then one said unto Him, Behold, Thy mother and Thy brethren stand without, desiring to speak with Thee. But He answered and said unto him that told Him, Who is My mother? And who are My brethren? And He stretched forth His hand toward His disciples, and said, Behold My mother and My brethren! For whosoever shall do the will of My Father which is in heaven, the same is My brother, and sister, and mother." [Matt. 12:46–50] On another occasion, when a woman said in adulation of His mother, "Blessed is the womb that bare Thee, and the paps which Thou hast sucked," His answer was: "Yea rather, blessed are they that hear the word of God, and keep it." [Luke 11:27, 28]

Jesus plainly stated that He was no respecter of persons, and that He esteemed in the same way all who obeyed Him.

The Roman Catholic Church lays great stress upon the salutation of the angel Gabriel when he said: "Blessed art thou among women." [Luke 1:28] But they overlook the fact that this was not the first time that God conferred a blessing upon a woman. About 1,300 years before the birth of Christ, a similar blessing was pronounced by divine inspiration upon a woman whose name was Jael. "Blessed above women shall Jael the wife of Heber the Kenite be, blessed shall she be above women." [Judg. 5:24] There is no intimation given in the word of God that this woman who is blessed "above" women was beatified or canonized. After a lapse of hundreds of years, Mary, who is blessed "among" women, is exalted by the Roman Church, and millions of worshipers are taught to bow at her shrine.

In answer to the question, "When was the blessed virgin canonized?" a well-known Jesuit periodical says: "The holy mother of God was never formally canonized, as we understand canonization today. Indeed, the first formal canonization probably does not go back farther than the tenth century, when Pope John XV solemnly canonized

The Wine of Roman Babylon

Saint Ulrich of Augsburg in A. D. 993....Finally, it was Urban VII who in a bull, published in 1634, reserved exclusively to the Holy See the right of beatification and canonization, which is the rule prevailing to this day.... Speaking to the book, neither the blessed virgin, John the Baptist, the twelve apostles, and numerous other early martyrs, were ever formally canonized, nor for that matter the archangels, though the cultus of all has been allowed by the [Roman] Church from the earliest times."[88]

When the truth of God is misconstrued, the Lord loses His rightful place as the center of worship, and the human mounts the throne. Thus it was in the case of those apostates "who changed the truth of God into a lie, and worshiped and served the creature more than the Creator." [Rom. 1:25] A papal doctor has said:

"Saint Basil of Seleucia declares that she [Mary] received this plenitude, that she might thus be a worthy mediatress between men and God: 'Hail, full of grace, mediatress between God and men, and by whom heaven and earth are brought together and united.' 'Otherwise,' says Saint Lawrence Justinian, 'had not the blessed virgin been full of divine grace, how could she have become the ladder to heaven, the advocate of the world, and the most true mediatress between men and God?'"[89]

Jesus spoke of Himself, not of His mother, as being the ladder to heaven, saying to Nathaniel:

"Verily, verily, I say unto you, Hereafter ye shall see heaven open, and the angels of God ascending and descending upon the Son of man." [John 1:51; Gen. 28:12]

Although John was given the guardianship of Mary by Christ, he knew nothing of the supposed honor of her office as mediatrix and advocate. This his own words testify: "My little children, these things write I unto you, that ye sin not. And if any man sin, we have an advocate

---

[88] *The Catholic Mind* (Jan. 1944) 61, 62.
[89] de Liguori, 294.

The Immaculate Conception

with the Father, Jesus Christ the righteous: and He is the propitiation for our sins: and not for ours only, but also for the sins of the whole world." [John 19:26, 27; 1 John 2:1, 2]

Neither did the apostle Paul know anything of the supposed intercessory work of Mary, as the following statement indicates: "For there is one God, and one mediator between God and men, the man Christ Jesus; who gave Himself a ransom for all, to be testified in due time." [1 Tim. 2:5, 6] If the communicants of the Roman Catholic Church were to accept the words of the apostle Paul, the following would never be uttered as to Mary:

> "Let us then cry out with Saint Thomas of Villanova, 'O Mary, we poor sinners know no other refuge than thee, for thou art our only hope, and on thee we rely for our salvation.' Thou art our only advocate with Jesus Christ; to thee we all turn ourselves."[90]

When the plan of redemption was first revealed in the garden of Eden, it carried with it the sentence pronounced upon Satan, and foretold the enmity which Christ would plant in the heart of man against sin. The Lord declared: "I will put enmity between thee and the woman, and between thy seed and her Seed; It [in Hebrew, "He shall bruise thy head, and thou shalt bruise His heel."[91]

We can realize the inexpressible joy and gratitude that filled the hearts of our first parents when they learned that the Son of God would offer Himself as an atonement for their sins. Yes, it took the One who was their Creator to be their Redeemer. The violation of the law of God could not be atoned for by the death of an angel, and much less by a human being. The Roman Catholic Church teaches that it was the woman, and not the promised Seed, who crushed the serpent's head. Here is its teaching:

---
[90] Ibid., 96.
[91] Gen. 3:15. The Hebrew text reads literally: "Enmity I shall put between thee and between the woman, and between thy seed and between her Seed; He shall crush thee a head, and thou shalt crush Him a heel."

> "It may be fairly alleged that the Bible begins with Mary. When God cursed the serpent, He said, 'I will put enmity between thee and the woman, and between thy seed and her seed.'...This prediction was fulfilled, and Mary received the highest dignity possible to a mere creature."[92]

Note the difference between the rendering of Genesis 3:15 in the Authorized Version and in the Douay Version: "And I will put enmity between thee and the woman, and between thy seed and her Seed; It shall bruise thy head, and thou shalt bruise His heel." Authorized Version. "I will put enmities between thee and the woman, and thy seed and her seed: she shall crush thy head, and thou shalt lie in wait for her heel." Douay Version. Is it not doing violence to the text to substitute "she" for "Seed" and "her" for "His"? The Sacred Scriptures expressly declare that the feat of crushing and destroying the devil and his angels is to be done by Christ Himself. "Forasmuch then as the children are partakers of flesh and blood, He also Himself likewise took part of the same; that through death He might destroy him that had the power of death, that is, the devil." [Heb. 2:14] "For this purpose the Son of God was manifested, that He might destroy the works of the devil." [1 John 3:8] "The God of peace shall bruise Satan under your feet shortly." [Rom. 16:20]

Contrary to the Sacred Scriptures, the papacy exalts Mary, saying:

> "It was indeed becoming that the three Divine Persons should preserve Mary from original sin. It was becoming that the Father should do so, because Mary was His first-born daughter. As Jesus was the first-born of God, 'the first-born of every creature,' so also was Mary, the destined mother of God, always considered by Him as His first-born daughter by adoption, and therefore He always possessed her by His grace: 'The Lord possessed me in the beginning of His ways.' For the honour, therefore, of His Son, it was

---

[92] Wm. E. Addis and Thomas Arnold, "Mary in Scripture," *A Catholic Dictionary*, 554.

The Immaculate Conception

becoming that the Father should preserve His mother from every stain of sin. It was also becoming that He should do so, because He destined this His daughter to crush the head of the infernal serpent, who had seduced man, as we read in Genesis, 'she shall crush thy head.' How, then, could He permit that she should first be the slave of this infernal serpent? Moreover, Mary was also destined to become the advocate of sinners; therefore it was also becoming that God should preserve her from sin, that she might not appear guilty of the same fault of men, for whom she was to intercede."[93]

Much has been written concerning Mary's death, assumption (ascension to heaven), and coronation as queen of heaven. The supposed miracles and supernatural events surrounding her demise cause the death of Christ to appear as a mere passing occurrence. Note carefully the following:

"This glorious death occurred on Friday the 13th of August, three hours before sunset, the age of the blessed mother being seventy years, wanting twenty-six days. This precious death was signalized by many miracles; the sun was eclipsed for a few hours; many birds entered into the dwelling, and by their plaintive cries, seemed to mourn the death of their queen; so remarkable were the evidences of their grief, that many were moved to tears. The whole city was filled with astonishment, and all confessed the power of the Almighty. Many of the sick were healed, and all the souls in purgatory were delivered, that they might accompany their merciful mother to heaven. At the same instant in which the virgin mother expired, three persons who dwelt near her also died, but in the unhappy state of mortal sin. When they appeared before the tribunal of Jesus Christ, the holy mother begged grace and mercy for them; they were allowed to return to life, and having done penance for their sins, happily persevered in grace and were saved."[94]

---
[93] de Liguori, 642, 643.
[94] Joseph A. Boullan, *The Life of the Blessed Virgin Mary* (New York: P. J. Kenedy & Sons) 420, 421.

The Wine of Roman Babylon

What happened during the supposed assumption procession from the tomb to heaven is astonishing. it is described thus:

"The magnificent procession departed from the sepulchre chanting celestial melodies, and ascended through the region of the air to the empyreal heaven. . . . Who is this that seems like the aurora, more beautiful than the moon, bright as the sun, and terrible as an army in battle array? Who is this that cometh up from the desert, leaning on her Beloved, and overflowing with delights? Who is this in whom the Divinity itself has found greater complacency than in all other creatures, and whom He has raised above all to the throne of His inaccessible light and, Majesty? O marvel, never before beheld in heaven! O prodigy of an omnipotent God, who thus glorifies and exalts her!

"Vested with this wonderful glory, the holy virgin arrived at the throne of the Divinity, and the three Divine Persons received her into their eternal and indissoluble embrace. She seemed as if absorbed within the three Divine Persons, and as if submerged in that infinite ocean of the abyss of the Divinity; the saints heard these words of the Eternal Father: 'Our daughter Mary has been elected and chosen by Our eternal will as the only and singular one among all creatures, and she is also the first in Our delights. She has never degenerated from her title of daughter, which in the divine understanding has been given her from all eternity; therefore she has a right to Our eternal kingdom, of which she is to be acknowledged and crowned the legitimate sovereign and queen.' The Incarnate Word said: 'To My true and natural mother belong all the creatures that I have created and redeemed, and all that I possess as king, she must also possess as legitimate queen.' The Holy Ghost said: 'By the title of My only and elected spouse, to which she has corresponded with perfect fidelity, the crown of queen is also due to her for all eternity.'

"After these words the three Divine Persons placed on the august head of the most holy virgin a crown of glory, which far exceeded any that ever has or ever shall be awarded to a creature. At the same instant a voice came from the throne,

The Immaculate Conception

saying: 'Our friend and Our chosen one among all other creatures, Our kingdom. belongs to thee. Thou art the sovereign, the queen and the mistress of the seraphim, the angels Our ministers, and of the entire creation. . . . Of the church militant thou art the empress, queen, mistress, protectress, advocate and mother. Thou shalt be the friend, patroness and protectress of all Our friends, the just. Console them, fortify and fill them with every good, if by their devotion they render themselves worthy. Thou art the depository of all Our divine benefits, the treasury of all Our graces. Into thy hands We remit the help and favor of Our grace, so that thou mayest dispense them; for We will grant nothing to the world but what shall pass through thy hands, and We will refuse nothing which thou mayest desire to grant. Grace shall be spread abroad on thy lips, for all that thou shalt wish and ordain in heaven and on earth; angels and men shall obey thee in all places, because all that is Ours belongs to thee, as thou hast always belonged to Us, and thou shalt reign with Us for all eternity.'

"For the execution of this eternal decree, the Omnipotent ordered all the heavenly court to render obedience and homage to her as their queen, and they promptly obeyed, acknowledging themselves her servants and vassals, and venerating her with a worship, filial fear, and respectful veneration like to that with which they adore the Lord."[95]

The Roman Church has conferred upon Mary authority that surpasses that of Christ, even going so far as to state that if Satan were to humble himself and seek her aid for salvation, she would be magnanimous enough to grant him pardon and thus convert him. Note this statement:

"The blessed virgin herself revealed to Saint Bridget 'that there is no sinner in the world, however much he may be at enmity with God, who does not return to Him and recover His grace, if he has recourse to her and asks her assistance.' The same Saint Bridget one day heard Jesus Christ address His mother, and say that 'she would be ready to obtain the grace of God for Lucifer himself, if only he humbled himself

---

[95] Ibid., 429–432.

The Wine of Roman Babylon

so far as to seek her aid.' That proud spirit will never humble himself so far as to implore the protection of Mary; but if such a thing were possible, Mary would be sufficiently compassionate, and her prayers would have sufficient power to obtain both forgiveness and salvation for him from God. But that which cannot be verified with regard to the devil is verified in the case of sinners who have recourse to this compassionate mother."[96]

After reading all this, should we not be thankful for the Holy Scriptures and the true Mediator, who alone can save the sinner? "For there is one God, and one Mediator between God and men, the man Christ Jesus; who gave Himself a ransom for all, to be testified in due time." [1 Tim. 2:5, 6] He became man, incarnated in human flesh, that He might represent us before the throne of the Deity. "Seeing then that we have a great High Priest, that is passed into the heavens, Jesus the Son of God, let us hold fast our profession. For we have not an high priest which cannot be touched with the feeling of our infirmities; but was in all points tempted like as we are, yet without sin. Let us therefore come boldly unto the throne of grace, that we may obtain mercy, and find grace to help in time of need." [Heb. 4:14–16] Although Mary was indeed a good woman, as otherwise God would never have entrusted to her care the rearing of Him who was to be our High Priest, it is not she who is to represent us before the throne of God, for "we have an advocate with the Father, Jesus Christ the righteous." [1 John 2:1] Those who believe the Holy Bible will give Christ His rightful place as the center of all worship. Never will they pay to another the homage that belongs to Him.

Also see the Appendix p. 217.

---

[96] de Liguori, 100.

CHAPTER XII

Invocation of Saints

HERE we shall analyze the eleventh sip of Babylon's wine, which we shall call "Invocation of Saints." The assumptious claim that the dead can be invoked for help in the hour of need, and for efficacious intercession in behalf of those who claim recourse to them, is unwarranted as far as the Written Word of God is concerned.

It is true that the Roman Catholic Church makes a distinction in the three degrees of worship, namely: latria, the form of worship due to God alone; hyperdulia the form of worship rendered to Mary, the mother of Jesus; and dulia, the form of worship which is given to the ecclesiastical saints and to angels. The worship of saints forms a very important part in the early religious life of a devout Roman Catholic. The special days set apart in honor of the saints are recognized. A deep regard is held for what the papal church teaches concerning certain saints who are supposed to preside over special blessings. St. Anthony's special mission is said to be to answer the prayers of the suppliant who has had the misfortune to lose some of his cherished possessions; St. Christopher's specialty is alleged to be to protect those who drive motor vehicles. A medal has been struck in his honor, and the bearer of one is thereby assured of the interposition of St. Christopher in time of danger.

A child is tempted to covet the honor conferred upon the saints by the Roman pope, and the veneration which they receive by the multitudes of Roman Catholics. I felt, when I was small, that no greater privilege could be accorded to a person than to be canonized as one of the Roman Catholic saints. Before canonization comes the stage of beatification. This is a solemn act by which the pope, after carefully scrutinizing the life, character, and services of the deceased person, declares him to be one of the blessed, and to have attained the degree of sanctity entitling him to certain public honors. This permits the dead saint to be venerated in a specified part of the church, and may lead to the final step of canonization, which entitles him to what is termed "the general veneration" of the church universal. It was not until the Middle Ages, however, that beatification was first introduced.

The act of canonization in the Roman Church is the culmination of a lengthy process. 'This ceremony is never performed until a period of at least fifty years has passed after the subject's death. The Congregation of Sacred Rites puts the prospective saint through various tests. Among the several alleged miracles credited to him, at least two must be proved to have taken place since his beatification. An exceedingly tedious inquiry is conducted with the most elaborate legal formalities; and after the testimony is given and the "evidence" of the miraculous power of the beatified saint has been proved, a favorable decision is pronounced by the pope. This ceremony is conducted with great pomp in St. Peter's Church at Rome. The first papal canonization that is recorded is that of Ulrich, bishop of Augsburg, by John XV in A. D. 993.

The beatifying and canonizing take on the form of litigation; and aside from the marriage annulment, in the Sacred Rota, there is none so lucrative in revenue. In order to have a person beatified, the rich relatives or friends of the deceased are obliged to employ a priest residing in Rome as their attorney, and he assumes the role of a postulator. Then, as the process takes on the form of a trial, somebody

Invocation of Saints

must be called to oppose the suit. This office is filled by a clerical lawyer known as the *promotor fidei*, who is otherwise called the "devil's advocate," because of the very nature of his official duties in connection with the canonization process.

Anyone familiar with the tribunals of Rome knows that it takes wealth coupled with influence to secure a favorable verdict in favor of canonization. It was about three centuries ago that the act of beatification became separate from that of canonization; and this, of course, serves to protract the litigation and thereby multiply the fees and costs which flow into the coffers of the Vatican.[97] Many legends have been written attesting to the diversities of miracles which have been wrought by these pope-made saints, and these tales are generally accepted as true by the laity without remonstrance. The reading of these stories fills the Roman Catholic with such veneration for these saints that one of his greatest delights is to repeat the litany of the saints.

Some of the papal saints receive more recognition than do others. Among the most distinguished ones is St. Joseph, who has been slowly ascending the mount of highly venerated human beings until today he is virtually accepted as the patron saint of the church universal. Says a Roman Catholic writer:

"St. Joseph occupies a place of his own in the devotion of modern [Roman] Catholics, such as is given to no other saint. This and the fact that the history of the devotion is peculiarly instructive on the one hand, specially liable to misunderstanding on the other, are the reasons for inserting this article in a work which does not profess to give lives of the

---

[97] "Beatification and Canonization," *The Catholic Encyclopedia* v2, 369. This article states that the expense of the public solemnities for the canonization of two dead men on May 15, 1897, by Leo XIII in the Church of St. Peter, in Rome, cost $42,816.87. The public solemnities, however, constitute only a small part of the total expenses involved in the whole process from start to finish.

The Wine of Roman Babylon

saints. The devotion to St. Joseph is a striking instance of [Roman] Catholic usage, modern in itself and yet based on most ancient and scriptural principles."[98]

It was as late as 1871 that the pope claimed to receive from heaven the authority to confer upon Joseph the rank of patron saint of the universal church. Thus we read:

"In 1871 Pius IX, confirming a decree of the Congregation of Rites, put the whole church under the patronage of St. Joseph, chose him as the church's protector, and made his feast a double of the first class. It was fitting that Christians should appeal to him who once protected the human life of our Saviour, and ask his intercession in behalf of Christ's mystical body. The same pope had in September, 1847, extended the feast and office of St. Joseph's patronage to the whole church."[99]

The whole month of March has been set aside and dedicated to the worship of Joseph, and numerous altars have been erected in his honor. For example:

"In other ways the church has marked her approval of the growing devotion to St. Joseph. The Creed is now said in the mass of both his feasts; his name is inserted after that of the blessed virgin in the prayer 'A cunctis;' he is commemorated after her in the suffrages of the saints; and his name comes before that of any other patron except the angels and St. John Baptist."[100]

The following statement taken from an authoritative Roman Catholic work clearly shows the position and the teaching of the papal church concerning the elevation of Joseph:

"'What angel or saint,' says Saint Basil, 'ever merited to be called the father of the Son of God? Joseph alone was thus called.' Hence we can well apply to Saint Joseph the words of Saint Paul, 'being made so much better than the angels, as he

---

[98] Wm. E. Addis and Thomas Arnold, "St. Joseph," *A Catholic Dictionary*, 485.
[99] Ibid., 486.
[100] Ibid.

Invocation of Saints

hath inherited a more excellent name than they.' Saint Joseph was more honored by God, in this name of father, than all the patriarchs, prophets, apostles, and pontiffs; for all these have tile name of servants, Joseph alone that of father."[101]

Has that church not gone beyond all bounds when she has taken the sacred words which God the Father addressed to His Son concerning His inherited name, and applied them to Joseph?

Another quotation sheds a little more light on how the Roman Church regards this patron saint:

"We should have a great confidence in the protection of Saint Joseph, because, on account of his sanctity, he was very dear to God."

"Saint Bernardine of Sienna adds, that 'we cannot doubt that Christ not only does not refuse to Saint Joseph in heaven that familiarity and reverence which, as a Son toward His father, He accorded him when He lived on earth, but rather, that it is now perfected.' Remark the words, familiarity and reverence; that Lord, who, on earth, revered Saint Joseph as His father, will certainly deny him nothing that he asks in heaven."[102]

"Let us now listen to what Saint Bernard writes of the power of Saint Joseph to dispense graces to his devout servants: 'To some of the saints power is granted to succor in particular necessities; but to Saint Joseph power is granted to succor in all necessities, and to defend all who, with devotion, have recourse to him.'...It would seem that to other saints our Lord has granted power to succor in some particular necessity; but experience proves that Saint Joseph succors in all. Of this we are certain; for, as on earth Jesus Christ was pleased to be subject to Saint Joseph, so in heaven He does all that the saint asks. Let us therefore imagine that we hear our Lord, when He sees us afflicted in the midst of our miseries, address us all in the words in which Pharaoh addressed his people at the time of the famine in Egypt: 'Go

---

101   de Liguori, 606.
102   Ibid., 611, 613.

The Wine of Roman Babylon

to Joseph, if you desire consolation.' By our Lord's grace, there is not at present a Christian in the world who is not devout to Saint Joseph; but, amongst them all, those receive the most abundant graces who recommend themselves to him the most frequently and with the greatest confidence. Let us therefore never pass a day without many times recommending ourselves to Saint Joseph who, after the most blessed virgin Mary, is the most powerful of all the saints with God. Let us never allow a day to pass without offering him some particular prayer; but especially during the novena for his feast, let us redouble our prayers, and fast on the vigil; and let us seek from him the graces which are useful for our souls; for he will always obtain them for us. In particular, I exhort you to ask for three special graces: for the forgiveness of your sins, the love of Jesus Christ, and a good death. As to the forgiveness of sins, I thus argue; when Jesus Christ lived in this world in the house of Saint Joseph, could a sinner who desired to obtain the forgiveness of his sins from our Lord, have found a more efficacious means to obtain this consolation than through Saint Joseph? If, then, we desire to be pardoned by God, let us have recourse to Saint Joseph, who, now that he is in heaven is more loved by Jesus Christ than he was loved by Him on earth....

"In the history of the discalced [barefooted] Carmelite it is also related that when the venerable Sister Anne of Saint Augustine, a Carmelite nun, was dying, some of her sisters saw Saint Joseph and Saint Teresa, who attended upon her, and that the servant of God was filled with joy. A nun in another convent saw her ascend to heaven between Saint Joseph and Saint Teresa. Father John de Allosa, in his book on Saint Joseph, relates, that a religious of the order of Saint Augustine appeared to a companion, and said, 'that God had delivered him from hell on account of the particular devotion which he had had for Saint Joseph.' He then declared that the saint, as the adopted father of Jesus Christ, had great power with Him."[103]

One can imagine what a person's mind is like after being under the tutorship of such teaching from infancy. But

---
[103] Ibid., 614–616.

Invocation of Saints

how contrary this teaching is to God and to His blessed word! That there is one pleader, or mediator, with God, the man Christ Jesus, is the emphatic declaration of the Inspired Book. [1 Tim. 2:5]

If Joseph were alive and could witness the homage which poor mortals are paying to him, he would assume, without a doubt, the same attitude the highest angel in heaven did when John fell at his feet to worship him. "And I fell at his feet to worship him. And he said unto me, See thou do it not: I am thy fellow servant, and of thy brethren that have the testimony of Jesus: worship God: for the testimony of Jesus is the spirit of prophecy."'

The angel not only forbade all worship to himself, but declared that worship is due only to God. This one text alone forever debars the invocation of saints. Anything that tends to usurp the worship due to Christ and to detract from His mediatorial work is not prompted from above but from beneath; for it is written: "There is one God, and one mediator between God and men, the man Christ Jesus." [Rev. 19:10]

The Holy Bible is significantly silent concerning the worship of the virgin Mary and the veneration of Peter, Paul, and other great men of the Christian faith. The Ten Commandments warn us against having other gods or bowing down to worship them. Is it not, therefore, a species of idolatry and a violation of the first and second commandments when worshipful veneration is given to men?

The Lord has given in the New Testament an example of a man who accepted the obeisance rendered him by his admirers. God's dealings with Herod, as recorded in the Book of Acts, are a reminder to us that He, the unchangeable One, will not allow idolatry to go unpunished. Pride and self-glory, the natural tendencies of the heart, soon develop when adulation is heaped upon a human being.

The Wine of Roman Babylon

When Herod appeared before the people to deliver his eloquent address, his wonderful oratory and majestic appearance charmed the assembly. As their gaze was transfixed on that mortal, they imagined they saw in him more than a human being, and exclaimed: "It is the voice of a god, and not of a man." [Acts 12:22] Herod's heart pulsated with pride as he heard these words. The God of heaven, looking down upon the idolatry committed by the people, and seeing the acceptance by Herod of the divine honors rendered him, was moved to immediate action by meting out divine retribution: "And immediately the angel of the Lord smote him, because he gave not God the glory: and he was eaten of worms, and gave up the ghost." [Acts 12:23] Thus ends the tragic episode of one who aspired to receive worshipful veneration.

The beatified and canonized saints are themselves unable to protest against the position to which the Roman Church has elevated them in her system of worship. If Mary, Joseph, Peter, and Paul were permitted to return from their graves to give their opinions concerning the Roman Catholic Church's teaching on the invocation of saints, would they not cry out in clarion tones against it? Peter, who while alive refused the worship which Cornelius respectfully offered him, would denounce most emphatically such doctrine, and would consummate his protests by having his name expunged from the papal list of canonized saints.

One species of idolatry leads to another, and this is certainly true when it comes to the worshiping of saints. The second commandment, as far as the Roman Catechism is concerned, practically does not exist. In my early life my attention was never called to the second commandment as given in the Holy Bible. If it had been, naturally the question would have arisen, Why all the images that meet the gaze of the worshipers as they enter the church? The omission of the second commandment of the Decalogue

Invocation of Saints

from most of the catechisms by which the Roman Catholic youth are taught tends to keep them in ignorance in regard to the prohibition that God makes against the forming and adoring of images. Here is the plain command of God: "Thou shalt not make unto thee any graven image, or any likeness of anything that is in heaven above, or that is in the earth beneath, or that is in the water under the earth: thou shalt not bow down thyself to them, nor serve them: for I the Lord thy God am a jealous God, visiting the iniquity of the fathers upon the children unto the third and fourth generation of them that hate Me: and showing mercy unto thousands of them that love Me and keep My commandments." [Exod. 20:4-6]

Among the many statements in Holy Writ relative to image-worship, there are none that stand out more forcibly than those found in the Book of Isaiah, where the Lord depicts the process which an image must go through in its manufacture. The Lord asks: "Is there a God beside Me? Yea, there is no God." [Isa. 44:8]

Time spent on making images, and worshiping them is more than wasted, as the ancient prophet reveals: "They that make a graven image are all of them vanity; and their delectable things shall not profit; and they are their own witnesses; they see not, nor know; that they may be ashamed. Who hath formed a god, or molten an image that is profitable for nothing?" [Isa. 44:9, 10]

In the case of idols made from metallic substances, the manufacturer necessarily must put the metal through a series of treatments before it is finished. This process is described in the Sacred Writings: "The smith with the tongs both worketh in the coals, and fashioneth it with hammers, and worketh it with the strength of his arms: yea, he is hungry, and his strength faileth: he drinketh no water, and is faint." [Isa. 44:12]

The Wine of Roman Babylon

The carpenter employs his skill in the making of objects of worship. The trees of the forest are cut down, and images of human form are made from them: "The carpenter stretcheth out his rule; he marketh it out with a line; he fitteth it with planes, and he marketh it out with the compass, and maketh it after the figure of a man, according to the beauty of a man; that it may remain in the house. He heweth him down cedars, and taketh the cypress and the oak, which he strengtheneth for himself among the trees of the forest: he planteth an ash, and the rain doth nourish it. Then shall it be for a man to burn: for he will take thereof, and warm himself; yea, he kindleth it, and baketh bread; yea, he maketh a god, and worshipeth it; he maketh it a graven image, and falleth down thereto." [Isa. 44:13-15]

The same tree which furnished material for the graven images which are to be worshiped, also supplies the maker with fuel to cook his food. "He burneth part thereof in the fire; with part thereof he eateth flesh; he roasteth roast, and is satisfied: yea, he warmeth himself, and saith, Aha, I am warm, I have seen the fire: and the residue thereof he maketh a god, even his graven image: he falleth down unto it, and worshipeth it, and prayeth unto it, and saith, Deliver me; for thou art my god." [Isa. 44:16, 17]

What can be more debasing to man than for him to adore and worship the object which his own hands have created? "What profiteth the graven image that the maker thereof hath graven it; the molten image, and a teacher of lies, that the maker of his work trusteth therein, to make dumb idols? Woe unto him that saith to the wood, Awake; to the dumb stone, Arise, it shall teach! Behold, it is laid over with gold and silver, and there is no breath at all in the midst of it." [Hab. 2:18, 19] "Their idols are silver and gold, the work of men's hands. They have mouths, but they speak not: eyes have they, but they see not: they have ears, but they hear not: noses have they, but they smell not: they have hands, but they handle not: feet have they, but they

Invocation of Saints

walk not: neither speak they through their throat. They that make them are like unto them: so is every one that trusteth in them." [Ps. 115:4-8]

The God of heaven, looking down upon the ignorant who invoke images of their own creation, is moved with tender compassion and sympathy. He longs to bring enlightenment to such benighted souls. The following words so full of pathos ought to bring a response from every heart. "O Israel, trust thou in the Lord: He is their help and their shield." [Ps. 115:9]

If God's word had been strictly obeyed, image-worship never would have been known. Note the instructions God gave to Israel: "Take ye therefore good heed unto yourselves; for ye saw no manner of similitude on the day that the Lord spake unto you in Horeb out of the midst of the fire: lest ye corrupt yourselves, and make you a graven image, the similitude of any figure, the likeness of male or female, the likeness of any beast that is on the earth, the likeness of any winged fowl that flieth in the air, the likeness of anything that creepeth on the ground, the likeness of any fish that is in the waters beneath the earth: and lest thou lift up thine eyes unto heaven, and when thou seest the sun, and the moon, and the stars, even all the host of heaven, shouldest be driven to worship them, and serve them, which the Lord thy God hath divided unto all nations." [Deut. 4:15-19]

The prayers, candles, and money offered in honor of the papal saints avail nothing, as the following apostolic statement indicates: "As concerning therefore the eating of those things that are offered in sacrifice unto idols, we know that an idol is nothing in the world, and that there is none other God but one....But to us there is but one God, the Father, of whom are all things, and we in Him; and one Lord Jesus Christ, by whom are all things, and we by Him." [1 Cor. 8:4, 6] Thus the apostle Paul was a decrier of

The Wine of Roman Babylon

idols. Were he alive today, he would give the Lord His rightful place and would denounce any infringement on the part of the human to usurp the prerogatives of God. Should we not stand with this illustrious soldier of Christ on this question?

The Son of God does not need the assistance of the Roman canonized saints to save and protect His creatures on earth, for "He is able also to save them to the uttermost that come unto God by Him, seeing He ever liveth to make intercession for them." [Heb. 7:25] How can anyone, after reading this statement from the word of God, refuse to give Christ His rightful position as our only intercessor with the Father?"

From what source did the Roman Catholic Church receive the doctrine of the invocation of saints? Why has this teaching been accepted with so much credulity? The answer is found in the assumption that the Roman Church and her teachings are infallible. Therefore, her dogmas are accepted by the masses without remonstrance. This doctrine, as well as many others of the papacy, was built upon tradition. This teaching of the invocation of saints was introduced first by Satan himself in the Garden of Eden, when he said: "Ye shall not surely die:…ye shall be as gods, knowing good and evil." [Gen. 3:4, 5] This was in direct contradiction to the command of God: "Ye shall not eat of it, neither shall ye touch it, lest ye die." [Gen. 3:3; 2:17] In Satan's statement, "Ye shall be as gods," we have the first step toward the beatification of saints, in which certain human beings were to be elevated to a position calling for veneration on the part of their fellow creatures.

Jesus Christ has gone through the portals of the tomb and has come forth a conqueror over death. Consequently, He can enlighten us on the question of where are the dead. In the words of Holy Writ this vital question is asked:

Invocation of Saints

"Man dieth, and wasteth away: yea, man giveth up the ghost, and where is he?" [Job 14:10]

Ask the Roman Catholic what his belief is in regard to one's condition and reward after death, and he will give the following answer based on tradition: "All receive their reward at death, as my church teaches that there is a heaven, a hell, a purgatory, and a limbo." Few Roman Catholics expect to go to heaven at death. Therefore the place of purification after death is the star of hope in the life of the conscientious Roman Catholic. Why do I call this a "star of hope"? Because the papal church offers means which not only is supposed to temper the fires of purgatory but also lessen the period of suffering for those who are confined in that place. This means was endorsed by the Council of Trent, and is still advocated tenaciously by the priesthood, who affirm "that there is a purgatory and that the souls detained there are benefited by the prayers of the faithful and especially by the acceptable sacrifice of the altar."[104]

In another Roman Catholic work we have the following questions and answers:

"Q. Where do those go who die with venial sins on their soul? A. Those who the with venial sins on their soul go to purgatory. Q. Who else go to purgatory? A. Those also who have not done enough penance for their sins go to purgatory. Q. Are those who go to purgatory saved? A. Those who go to purgatory are saved....Q. Can we help the souls in purgatory? A. We can help the souls in purgatory by praying for them, by having masses said for them, and by gaining certain indulgences for them."[105]

The Roman Catholic Church also emphasizes the importance of having recourse to the virgin Mary. It is alleged that her continual intercession, merits, special protection, and occasional visits to those suffering ones

---
[104] Martin, 288, 289.
[105] MacEachen, 56.

The Wine of Roman Babylon

add hope and consolation to the living who petition Mary in behalf of their deceased loved ones. It is said, for example:

"The divine mother once addressed these words to Saint Bridget: 'I am the mother of all souls in purgatory; for all the pains that they have deserved for their sins are every hour, as long as they remain there, in some way mitigated by my prayers.' The compassionate mother even condescends to go herself occasionally into that holy prison, to visit and comfort her suffering children. Saint Bonaventure, applying to Mary the words of Ecclesiasticus, 'I have penetrated into the bottom of the deep,' says, 'the deep, that is, purgatory, to relieve by my presence the holy souls detained there.' 'O, how courteous and benign is the most blessed virgin,' says Saint Vincent Ferrer, 'to those who suffer in purgatory! Through her they constantly receive comfort and refreshment.'...The mere name of Mary, that name of hope and salvation, and which is frequently invoked by her beloved children in their prison, is a great source of comfort to them; 'for,' says Novarinus, 'that loving mother no sooner hears them call upon her than she offers her prayers to God, and these prayers, as a heavenly dew, immediately refresh them in their burning pains.'"[106]

What consolation is held out to the living by the many legends told of Mary's untiring intercessory work in behalf of those who are her clients, the following narrative reveals:

"In the year 1604, in a city of Flanders, there were two young men, students, but who, instead of attending to their studies, gave themselves up to a life of debauchery. One night they were both in a house with an evil companion, when one of them, named Richard, returned home, leaving his companion there. After he got home, and had begun to undress, he remembered he had not that day said some 'Hail Marys' that he was in the habit of reciting. Feeling very sleepy he was loth to say them; he did himself violence, and repeated them, though without devotion, and half asleep.

---
[106] de Liguori, 206, 207.

He then lay down, and had fallen into a sound slumber, when he was suddenly roused by a violent knocking at the door, and without its opening he saw his companion, deformed and hideous, standing before him. 'Who art thou?' he cried out. 'What! dost thou not know me?' 'Ah, yes! but how thou art changed; thou seemest to me a devil.' 'Truly,' he exclaimed, 'poor unfortunate creature that I am, I am damned; and how? When I was leaving that wicked house a devil came and strangled me: my body is in the street, and my soul in hell; and thou must know,' added he, 'that the same fate awaited thee, had not the blessed virgin preserved thee in consideration of that little act of homage of the "Hail Mary." Fortunate art thou if only thou knowest how to take advantage of this warning sent thee by the mother of God.' With these words he opened his mantle, and, showing the flames and serpents by which he was tormented, he disappeared. Richard immediately burst into sobs and tears, and, casting himself prostrate on the ground, he returned thanks to Mary, his protectress; and, whilst thinking how to change his life, he heard the bell of the Franciscan monastery ringing for matins. 'Ah! it is there,' says he, 'that God calls me to do penance.' He went straight off to the convent, and implored the fathers to admit him. But they were hardly willing to do so, knowing his wicked life; but he, sobbing bitterly, told all that had taken place; and two fathers being sent to the street, and having found the strangled body, which was as black as a coal, they admitted him. From that time forward Richard led a most exemplary life, and at length went to preach the gospel in the Indies, and thence to Japan, where he had the happiness of giving his life for Jesus Christ, being burnt alive for the faith."[107]

Another excerpt taken from the same author reveals the supposed plenitude of Mary's power to release all souls found in purgatory at the time of her assumption:

"Mary not only consoles and relieves her clients in purgatory, but she delivers them by her prayers. Gerson says, 'that on the day of her assumption into heaven purgatory was entirely emptied.' Novarinus confirms this, saying, 'that it is

---

[107] Ibid., 202-204.

maintained by many grave authors, that when Mary was going to heaven, she asked, as a favor from her Son, to take all the souls then in purgatory with her.' 'And from that time forward,' says Gerson, 'Mary had the privilege of delivering her servants.' Saint Bernardine of Sienna also positively asserts, 'that the blessed virgin has the power of delivering souls from purgatory, but particularly those of her clients, by her prayers, and by applying her merits for them.' Novarinus says, 'that by the merits of Mary, not only are the pains of those souls lessened, but the time of their sufferings is shortened through her intercession.' She has only to ask, and all is done."[108]

"Fortunate, indeed, are the clients of this most compassionate mother; for not only does she succor them in this world, but even in purgatory they are helped and comforted by her protection. And as in that prison poor souls are In the greatest need of assistance, since in their torments they cannot help themselves, our mother of mercy does proportionately more to relieve them. Saint Bernardine of Sienna says, 'that in that prison, where souls which are spouses of Jesus Christ are detained, Mary has a certain dominion and plenitude of power, not only to relieve them, but even to deliver them from their pains.'"[109]

We ask the Protestant, who claims to have the written word of God for the foundation of all his religious belief, "What is your belief as to where a man goes after death?" His answer often is: "I believe that at the time of death a man goes either to heaven or to hell."

Let us lay aside all preconceived ideas and prejudices in regard to the great question of where are the dead, and with an unbiased mind listen to what God has to say on this vital subject. The Holy Scriptures declare that at death a man goes into the grave and will remain there until his resurrection comes. "If I wait, the grave is mine house: I have made my bed in the darkness," [Job 17:13] said Job. And he says also: "So man lieth down, and riseth not: till

---

[108] Ibid., 207.
[109] Ibid., 205.

the heavens be no more, they shall not awake, nor be raised out of their sleep. O that Thou wouldest hide me in the grave, that Thou wouldest keep me secret, until Thy wrath be past, that Thou wouldest appoint me a set time, and remember me! If a man die, shall he live again? All the days of my appointed time will I wait, till my change come. Thou shalt call, and I will answer Thee: Thou wilt have a desire to the work of Thine hands." [Job 14:12–15]

The voice of the Son of God, at His second coming, will awaken the sleeping saints and bring them forth from the grave. "Marvel not at this: for the hour is coming, in the which all that are in the graves shall hear His voice, and shall come forth; they that have done good, unto the resurrection of life; and they that have done evil, unto the resurrection of damnation." [John 5:28, 29]

It is at the resurrection of the righteous that immortality is to be conferred. "Behold, I show you a mystery: We shall not all sleep, but we shall all be changed, in a moment, in the twinkling of an eye, at the last trump: for the trumpet shall sound, and the dead shall be raised incorruptible, and we shall be changed." [1 Cor. 15:51, 52]

The trump of God, which shall awaken the dead, has not yet sounded, because the second coming of Christ is a future event. Job looked forward to the day when he would see God in his flesh, thus showing that he believed in the resurrection of the body. "For I know that my Redeemer liveth, and that He shall stand at the latter day upon the earth: and though after my skin worms destroy this body, yet in my flesh shall I see God: whom I shall see for myself, and mine eyes shall behold, and not another; though my reins be consumed within me." [Job 19:25–27]

God's word refutes the theory that when a man dies he is still alive, and that the dead know more than when they were alive. "For the living know that they shall die: but *the dead know not anything*, neither have they any more a

The Wine of Roman Babylon

reward; for the memory of them is forgotten." [Eccles. 9:5] A person who is dead is incapable of either loving or hating. "Also their love, and their hatred, and their envy, is now perished; neither have they any more a portion forever in anything that is done under the sun." [Eccles. 9:6]

One could never dwell in the atmosphere of heaven and not give praise to the Lord. Hence we are told that "the dead praise not the Lord, neither any that go down into silence." [Ps. 115:17] Could anyone be in heaven and forget God? Never! Those who go down in death do not remember their Lord. "For in death there is no remembrance of Thee: in the grave who shall give Thee thanks?" [Ps. 6:5] "Death is called a "land of forgetfulness." "Wilt thou show wonders to the dead? Shall the dead arise and praise Thee? Selah. Shall Thy lovingkindness be declared in the grave? Or Thy faithfulness in destruction? Shall Thy wonders be known in the dark? And Thy righteousness in the land of forgetfulness?" [Ps. 88:10-12]

When the breath leaves the human body, all the physical machinery ceases to function, rendering the brain incapable of producing thoughts. "Put not your trust in princes, nor in the son of man, in whom there is no help. His breath goeth forth, he returneth to his earth; *in that very day his thoughts perish.*" [Ps. 146:3, 4]

The prayers offered to Mary and all the other deceased saints fall upon dead ears. The enemy of our souls knew what he was doing when he accosted Eve in the Garden of Eden and told her this lie, "Ye shall not surely die." [Gen. 3:4] Who would have thought that these few contradictory words by Satan could produce such a monument of fabrication that almost the whole world — not only heathen and Roman Catholics, but even Protestants — would accept them!

Invocation of Saints

Clergymen have officiated at funerals and read portions from the Holy Scriptures concerning the resurrection of the dead. On closing the Inspired Book, they would proceed to bring comfort to the bereaved family by eulogizing the dead and speaking of them as being in heaven, thus contradicting all they had read from the Sacred Tome. David, of whom God said, "I have found David the son of Jesse, a man after Mine own heart, which shall fulfill all My will," [Acts 13:22] did not go to heaven when he died. About 1,000 years after David's death, the apostle Peter himself made this statement: "Men and brethren, let me freely speak unto you of the patriarch David, that he is both dead and buried, and his sepulcher is with us unto this day....For David is not ascended into the heavens." [Acts 2:29, 34] Just as David is sleeping in his grave, so all those who have died down through the ages and have not been raised from the dead are likewise reposing in earth's bosom.

The term "soul" is a much distorted word in the circles of theology, and around it have risen numerous and conflicting ideas. The generality of people believe that they *have* souls. Hence we may properly ask, "What is the soul?" We read that at creation "the Lord God formed man of the dust of the ground, and breathed into his nostrils the breath of life; and man *became* a living soul." [Gen. 2:7] This does not say that man *has* a soul, but that he *is* one.

This word "soul" in the Hebrew tongue is *nephesh*, which is translated "creature" in the following passage: "And God said, Let the earth bring forth the living creature [*nephesh*] after his kind, cattle, and creeping thing, and beast of the earth after his kind." [Gen. 1:24] "It is also translated as "creature" in Genesis 1: 20, where the term is applied to the fish and the fowl. In the New Testament we have the word "soul" applied to creatures of the sea. "And the second angel poured out his vial upon the sea; and it became as the blood of a dead man - and every living soul died in the sea." [Rev. 16:3]

One may ask about the spirit that God placed within man in the beginning, and wish to know what becomes of it at death. First, let the Lord tell us what this spirit is, bow it was given, and in what part of the body it was placed. God "formed man of the dust of the ground." Although his body was perfect, it was lifeless. Every organ was motionless until God breathed life into the body. God "breathed into his nostrils the breath of life." [Gen. 2:7]

In the Book of Job the Lord defines the breath of life as "the spirit." Note these words: "All the while my breath is in me, and the spirit of God is in my nostrils." [Job 27:3] The margin reads: "The breath which God gave him." When the breath, or spirit, leaves the body, a man dies. Thus it is with the beast, for the same kind of breath that gives life to man also gives life to the beast. "For that which befalleth the sons of men befalleth beasts; even one thing befalleth them: as the one dieth, so dieth the other; yea, they have all one breath; so that a man hath no preeminence above a beast: for all is vanity. All go unto one place; all are of the dust, and all turn to dust again. Who knoweth the spirit of man that goeth upward, and the spirit of the beast that goeth downward to the earth?" [Eccles. 3:19-21]

While the breath of the beast goes down and perishes, that of man is preserved by the Creator. "Then shall the dust return to the earth as it was: and the spirit shall return unto God who gave it." [Eccles. 12:7]

In the great resurrection of the dead the breath of life will be restored to the body. The prophet Ezekiel gives a graphic description of the reality of the resurrection of the dead from the grave. He records his vision thus:

"The hand of the Lord was upon me, and carried me out in the Spirit of the Lord, and set me down in the midst of the valley which was full of bones, and caused me to pass by them round about: and, behold, there were very many in the open valley; and, lo, they were very dry. And He said unto me, Son of man, can these bones live? And I answered, O Lord God, Thou knowest. Again He said unto me, Prophesy upon these bones, and say unto them, O ye dry bones, hear the word of the Lord. Thus saith the Lord God unto these bones; Behold, I will cause breath to enter into you, and ye shall live: and I will lay sinews upon you, and will bring up flesh upon you, and cover you with skin, and put breath in you, and ye shall live; and ye shall know that I am the Lord. So I prophesied as I was commanded: and as I prophesied, there was a noise, and behold a shaking, and the bones came together, bone to his bone. And when I beheld, lo, the sinews and the flesh came up upon them, and the skin covered them above: but there was no breath in them. Then said He unto me, Prophesy unto the wind, prophesy, son of man, and say to the wind, Thus saith the Lord God; Come from the four winds, O breath, and breathe upon these slain, that they may live. So I prophesied as He commanded me, and the breath came into them, and they lived, and stood up upon their feet, an exceeding great army. Then He said unto me, Son of man, these bones are the whole house of Israel: behold, they say, Our bones are dried, and our hope is lost: we are cut off for our parts. Therefore prophesy and say unto them, Thus saith the Lord God: Behold, O My people, I will open your graves, and cause you to come up out of your graves, and bring you into the land of Israel. And ye shall know that I am the Lord, when I have opened your graves, O My people, and brought you up out of your graves, and shall put My Spirit in you, and ye shall live, and I shall place you in your own land: then shall ye know that I the Lord have spoken it, and performed it, saith the Lord." [Ezek. 37:1-14]

The Wine of Roman Babylon

This prophecy portrays very vividly the scene of the resurrection. Note that the breath coming in contact with the body will give it life.

Surely the erroneous doctrine of life after death has paved the way for many false doctrines, such as the beatification and invocation of Mary and the saints, the sacrifice of the mass in behalf of the dead, purgatory, the limbus infantium, and infant baptism. These doctrines have been used by the Roman Church to delude poor souls and to enrich her treasury.

It is not by relying upon the interposition of the human that divine merits are secured. It is through Christ alone that infinite love and mercy are obtained. It is because fallen men can do nothing for themselves that Jesus died, and it is His sacrifice alone that restores the human family to God. Instead of trusting in the supposed merits and favors of canonized saints, let us trust in the merits of our crucified and risen Saviour. "Neither is there salvation in any other: for there is none other name under heaven given among men, whereby we must be saved." [Acts 4:12]

Also see the Appendix p. 221.

CHAPTER XIII

Immortality of the Soul

AGAIN we approach the cup of Babylon's wine and draw from it the doctrine of "Immortality of the Soul," which is the twelfth sip. The belief and teaching of the Roman Catholic Church. is that man is inherently immortal, and that after death he lives on in the form of an immortal soul. This doctrine has given birth to numerous false ideas concerning the state of man after death, and has been adopted by most of the Protestant sects. Do the Sacred Scriptures teach that man now possesses an immortal soul?

The word "immortal" occurs only once in our Authorized (King James') Version of the Bible, and in this instance it refers to God alone. "Now unto the King eternal, immortal, invisible, the only wise God, be honor and glory forever and ever. Amen." [1 Tim. 1:17] If all men were now invested with immortality, surely the word of God would not be silent about it. But it clearly states that only God has immortality. "Which in His times He shall show, who is the blessed and only Potentate, the King of kings, and Lord of lords; *who only hath immortality*, dwelling in the light which no man can approach unto; whom no man hath seen, nor can see: to whom be honor and power everlasting. Amen." [1 Tim. 6:15, 16]

Eternal life is promised on condition that we accept Christ, and those who do not meet this condition cannot have eternal life. "And this is the record, that God hath given to us eternal life, and this life is in His Son. He that hath the Son hath life; and he that hath not the Son of God hath not life. [1 John 5:11, 12] Christ assures us that it is through the belief in, and adherence to, the word of God that we receive immortality. "Verily, verily, I say unto you, He that heareth My word, and believeth on Him that sent Me, hath everlasting life, and shall not come into condemnation; but is passed from death unto life." [John 5:24] If we were innately the possessors of immortality, we would not have to be admonished to seek for it. But Paul says that "eternal life" will be the reward "to them who by patient continuance in well doing seek for glory and honor and immortality." [Rom. 2:7]

The Lord does not leave us in doubt as to where and how immortality can be obtained. The gospel, which reveals Jesus Christ, is proclaimed in the Holy Scriptures. Therefore, by the study of, and faithful obedience to, their divine teachings we may have immortality bestowed on us at the second coming of Christ, for our Saviour "hath abolished death, and hath brought life and immortality to light through the gospel." [2 Tim. 1:10] "When Christ, who is our life, shall appear, then shall ye also appear with Him in glory." [Col. 3:4]

Not until incorruption shall take the place of corruption, and mortality shall give way to immortality, will eternal life be ours. "So when this corruptible shall have put on incorruption, and this mortal shall have put on immortality, then shall be brought to pass the saying that is written, Death is swallowed up in victory." [1 Cor. 15:54] Loving life, as we do, and knowing that immortality will not be granted until the second coming of Jesus Christ, we ought to prepare for, and look forward to, that glorious event. In the beginning, when man yielded to sin, he forfeited the right to eternal life. [Gen. 3:22–24] It is only through faith in Christ and His atonement that man regains his sinless state of character and the right to immortality. "For God so loved the world, that He gave His only-begotten Son, that whosoever believeth in Him should not perish, but have everlasting life." [John 3:16]

The Lord was too wise to mete out eternal fife to everyone, to saint and to sinner alike. He demonstrated His divine wisdom when He banished Adam and Eve from the Garden of Eden after they had sinned, thus preventing them from partaking of the tree whose properties would perpetuate life. "And the Lord God said, Behold, the man is become as one of us, to know good and evil: and now, lest he put forth his hand, and take also of the tree of life, and eat, and live for ever: therefore the Lord God sent him forth from the garden of Eden, to till the ground from whence he was taken. So He drove out the man; and He placed at the east of the garden of Eden cherubims, and a flaming sword which turned every way, to keep the way of the tree of life." [Gen. 3:22-24]

If man had been permitted access to the tree of life after his disobedience, he would have become an immortal sinner and not be subject to death. If all sinners of the past millenniums were alive today with their years of experience in sin, what a terrible world this would be to live in! To safeguard society our courts of justice mete out death or imprisonment to violators of the civil law. Now suppose that they were dealing with immortal criminals, who could never die. If they should attempt to exclude them from society by placing them in penal institutions, the world would not have room enough for buildings in which to incarcerate them. Some may say: "That is too preposterous for words!" However, that is exactly what the law enforcers would be confronted with, if it were true that men are immortal. Although death is our enemy, it has made this sinful world a safer place in which to live.

Had Adam and Eve been obedient to God, they would have continued to eat of the fruit of the tree of life, and would have lived forever; but when they disobeyed and broke God's commandment, they were cut off from partaking of this life-giving fruit, and thus became subject to death. God never has promised eternal life to the disobedient. However, Satan in his declaration to Eve, "Ye shall not surely die," has promised men life through disobedience. Thus the first sermon ever preached on the doctrine of the immortality of the soul was spoken by the devil. These words uttered by the enemy of truth have been echoed and re-echoed from pagan, Protestant, and Roman Catholic pulpits, and the majority of mankind have embraced with complacency this false doctrine.

The plan of salvation will reach its culmination when the redeemed will be taken home to the glory land, where God's commandment-keeping children will receive the royal welcome of King Jesus. Then He will grant them the happy privilege of partaking of the life-perpetuating fruit from which man has been so long excluded. "Blessed are they that do His commandments, that they may have right to the tree of life, and may enter in through the gates into the city." [Rev. 22:14] The condition upon which eternal life is granted stands the same today as it did when Christ answered the rich young ruler's question: "What good thing shall I do, that I may have eternal life?" The answer was: "If thou wilt enter into life, keep the commandments." [Matt. 19:16, 17] Peter said: "Repent, and be baptized every one of you in the name of Jesus Christ for the remission of sins." [Acts 2:38] The apostles also said: "Repent ye therefore, and be converted, that your sins may be blotted out." [Acts 3:19] Paul said: "Believe on the Lord Jesus Christ, and thou shalt be saved." [Acts 16:31] In other words, obedience as well as faith, conversion, and baptism are needed.

Stop sipping from the cup which contains the erroneous doctrine of inherent immortality. Accept God's words, by His grace obey His commandments, and have implicit faith in the full atonement of Jesus Christ. "This do, and thou shalt live." [Luke 10:28]

Also see the Appendix p. 223.

Above—This photo shows men confessing to priests in the open-air confessional at Lourdes. These penitents are of a group of 45,000 persons who made a pilgrimage to the shrine. (Photo by International News.)

Below—Although the Roman Catholic confessional usually is a closet or box divided into two parts, with a screen opening in the partition, open confessionals are used for special occasions. Every Roman Catholic is required by his church to confess at least once a year. (Photo by Acme.)

CHAPTER XIV

Eternal Torment in Hell

AGAIN we examine the cup of Babylon, and the thirteenth draught drawn from it is the doctrine of "Eternal Torment in Hell." Here is what the Roman Catholic Church teaches about hell: "Hell may be defined as the place and state in which the devils and such human beings as die in enmity with God suffer eternal torments."[110]

After his fall Satan made every effort possible to inculcate in man belief in the doctrine of natural immortality. Having succeeded in persuading men to accept this false doctrine, he then led them to the conclusion that after death sinners are consigned to and confined in a place of eternal misery called "hell." The devil has worked through this doctrine to misrepresent God, and thus he has led multitudes to regard Him as a cruel, avenging, despotic tyrant instead of a kind, merciful, and loving Father. This teaching pictures God as an inflexible tyrant seeking revenge on those who disobey Him, and consigning them to an eternal inferno to suffer unutterable anguish throughout the endless ages of eternity. The propagation of such a teaching, which is designed by the enemy to lead many away from God and to give rise to atheism, has caused multitudes to be lost.

Our whole being should recoil at the thought of an infinite God assigning one of His creatures, one who has lived such a brief period of time on this earth, to a lake of

---

[110] Wm. E. Addis and Thomas Arnold, "Hell," *A Catholic Dictionary,* 395.

The Wine of Roman Babylon

fire to burn, scorch, and sizzle throughout eternity. The stories told by the popular theologians, in which they depict the existing anguish of miserable souls in hell, awaken both wrath and pity in the heart of the most adamant—wrath against a God who would be responsible for such a horrible mode of perpetual torture; and pity for the unfortunate victims of such cruel bondage and suffering.

Where in the word of God can such a teaching be found? Not within the covers of the Holy Bible. It was instituted by Satan, and has been propagated by pagan and papal Rome, and the refrain has been picked up by Protestant ministers, until it is sounded all over Christendom and accepted by millions of credulous people, Can anyone picture a loving God taking delight in the smoke of an endless inferno, and having an everlasting reminder of sin to blight His fair universe? Never!

The words of Ezekiel emphatically set forth God's attitude toward the violation of His holy law, and His displeasure over the death of the wicked: "Say unto them, As I live, saith the Lord God, I have no pleasure in the death of the wicked; but that the wicked turn from his way and live: turn ye, turn ye from your evil ways; for why will ye die, O house of Israel?" [Ezek. 33:11] Instead of desiring to confine a person in endless misery, the Holy Bible pictures our God as one who is full of love, abounding in goodness and mercy. Would the redeemed enjoy the bliss of heaven knowing that one of their loved ones was in a place of ceaseless torment? The doctrine of an everlasting hell, and its accompanying theories, are the component parts of that intoxicating cup from which the religious world has drunk.

The word "hell," translated from the Hebrew word *sheol*, occurs sixty-five times in the Old Testament and means "grave" or "pit." One authority says: "This [hell] is the word generally used by our translators to render the Hebrew *sheol*. It would perhaps have been better to retain the Hebrew word *sheol*, or else render it always by 'the grave' or 'the pit.'"[111]

Let us consider the three Greek words *hades*, *geenna*, and *tartaroō*, which are translated as "hell" in the Authorized Version of the New Testament. The Greek word *hades* is translated "hell" ten times, and "grave" once, in the New Testament. The term means, "the unseen" and is properly translated "grave," where the deceased are laid away and put out of sight. Instead of the grave, or "hell," being a place of punishment for the wicked, it is one of rest.

"Whatsoever thy hand findeth to do, do it with thy might; for there is no work, nor device, nor knowledge, nor wisdom, in the grave, whither thou goest." [Eccles. 9:10]

Hell has been pictured by the theologians as a yawning abyss of flaming fire, where Satan with his pitchfork is supposed to keep vigil over his tormented prisoners. God's word, on the other hand, gives an entirely different picture of hell from that which is depicted by the papists. It says: "There the wicked cease from troubling; and there the weary be at rest. There the prisoners rest together; they hear not the voice of the oppressor. The small and great are there; and the servant is free from his master." [Job 3:17–19]

If dead sinners were suffering in a lake of fire, there certainly would be no "rest" there for the "weary." Note that, too, "the servant is free from his master." If the devil were given authority over the wicked dead, freedom would never be granted to any of his subjects, for he is the author of slavery.

The Book of Acts states that Christ's soul was not left in "hell" (*hades*) long enough for His flesh to see corruption, In the Psalms it was written of Him: "For Thou wilt not

---
111 William Smith, "Hell," *A Dictionary of the Bible*, 234.

leave My soul in hell; neither wilt Thou suffer Thine Holy One to see corruption." And commenting on this, Peter said: "He seeing this before spake of the resurrection of Christ, that His soul was not left in hell, neither His flesh did see corruption." [Ps. 16:8–10; Acts 2:27–31]

Can anyone imagine Christ being consigned to a place of burning while He was dead? Certainly God knows where man goes at death. "For that which befalleth the sons of men befalleth beasts; even one thing befalleth them: as the one dieth, so dieth the other; yea, they have all one breath; so that a man hath no pre-eminence above a beast: for all is vanity. All go unto one place; all are. of the dust, and all turn to dust again." [Eccles. 3: 19, 20]

Thus the Written Word gives no support to the belief in, and doctrine of, a present place of punishment where the unsaved dead are confined and tortured. The hades, or "hell," to which the Sacred Scriptures refer is the grave where dead saints and dead sinners are resting until the resurrection day, when the just will be raised to eternal life, and the sinners will come forth to eternal death. [John 5:28, 29] The doctrine of an everlasting hell of torment in flames is repugnant to all human feeling, and must be much more so to the God of infinite love and mercy.

The Greek word *geenna* refers to a place of burning, and is used twelve times in the New Testament.[112] The term itself is a proper noun which means "Valley of Hinnom." In these where the term is found, it is clearly seen that there is a place where the ungodly shall be punished for their sins, but nowhere do the texts, indicate that such punishment will be protracted by endless confinement in a lake of fire that can never burn out. The Gehenna, to which Jesus referred as an illustration of the place where the wicked shall be punished, was the valley of Hinnom lying on the

---

112 Matt. 5:22, 29, 30; 10:28; 18:9; 23:15, 33; Mark 9:43, 45, 47; Luke 12:5; James 3:6.

Eternal Torment in Hell

south side of Jerusalem. There human sacrifices were offered to the god Moloch in ancient times [2 Chron. 33:6] but in the days of Christ, it was used as a place where the refuse of the city was burned up. The fires of Hinnom continued to burn as long as any particle of refuse remained.

We can understand what the destruction of the wicked will be like, for it is described by Christ by the use of the illustration comparing their end to burning in Gehenna just outside the city of ancient Jerusalem. It will be outside of the city of the New Jerusalem that the violators of God's law will receive their wages. "And [the devil] shall go out to deceive the nations which are in the four quarters of the earth, Gog and Magog, to gather them together to battle; the number of whom is as the sand of the sea. And they went up on the breadth of the earth, and compassed the camp of the saints about, and the beloved city: and fire came down from God out of heaven, and devoured them." [Rev. 20:8, 9] just as the fires of Gehenna anciently became extinguished after fulfilling their purpose in consuming every piece of refuse, so the Gehenna of the last days will be quenched when the complete annihilation of the wicked shall have taken place. The same language used in reference to the unquenchable fire which is to destroy the wicked, is used also in speaking of the destruction of Jerusalem in days of old. "But if ye will not harken unto Me to hallow the Sabbath day, and not to bear a burden, even entering in at the gates of Jerusalem on the Sabbath day; then will I kindle a fire in the gates thereof, and it shall devour the palaces of Jerusalem, and it shall not be quenched." [Jer. 17:27]

God visited the ancient city of Jerusalem with unquenchable fire at the hands of the armies of Babylon. [2 Kings 25:9, 10; 2 Chron. 36:19; Isa. 64:11] No one could stay the hand of the destroyer until the utter destruction of that city was accomplished. Thus it will be when the Lord shall mete out final punishment to the unsaved by means of unquenchable fire, which will be everlasting in its effect. The word of God declares that Sodom and Gomorrah were visited with "eternal fire," but these cities are not burning today. Jude speaks of "Sodom and Gomorrah, and the cities about them in like manner, giving themselves over to fornication, and going after strange flesh, are set forth for an example, suffering the vengeance of eternal fire." [Jude 7]

These words "everlasting," "eternal," "unquenchable," when used by God in referring to the reward of the wicked, mean that the punishment will be eternal in its effect, and nowhere do they convey the idea that there will not be a finality to their suffering. It is eternal punish*ment* and not endless punish*ing* that will be the fate of the wicked. "And these shall go away into everlasting punishment: but the righteous into life eternal." [Matt. 25:46] It is to "everlasting destruction," and not to everlasting life in a place of misery, that the word of God teaches that the wicked are destined to go. They "shall be punished with everlasting destruction from the presence of the Lord, and from the glory of His power." [2 Thess. 1:9] Man does not innately possess eternal life; it is a gift from God. [John 3:16; Rom. 6:23] Can anyone imagine a God of love giving the gift of eternal life to any of His creatures for the purpose of punishing them with indescribable suffering throughout eternity in an inferno? It is death, and not life, that is to be the portion of the transgressors of the divine law. The death resulting from sin will be the "second death." "And the sea gave up the dead which were in it; and death and hell ["grave," margin] delivered up the dead which were in them: and they were judged every man according to their works. And death and hell were cast into the lake of fire. This is the second death." [Rev. 20:13, 14] "But the fearful, and unbelieving, and the abominable, and murderers, and whoremongers, and sorcerers, and idolators, and all liars, shall have their part in the lake which burneth with fire and brimstone: which is the second death." [Rev. 21:8] "For the wages of sin is death; but the gift of God is eternal life through Jesus Christ our Lord." [Rom. 6:23] Therefore death will be the fate of the impenitent.

Even the soul itself will perish, for it is written: "The soul that sinneth, it shall die." [Ezek. 18:4, 20]

The wicked are likened in Holy Writ to stubble, which is something easily consumed and reduced to ashes. "For, behold, the day cometh, that shall burn as an oven; and all the proud, yea, and all that do wickedly, shall be stubble: and the day that cometh shall burn them up, saith the Lord of hosts, that it shall leave them neither root nor branch.... And ye shall tread down the wicked; for they shall be ashes under the soles of your feet in the day that I shall do this, saith the Lord of hosts." [Mal. 4:1, 3]

These texts clearly state that there is nothing asbestine about the sinner to prevent his complete destruction in the final punishment. The place where the wicked and Satan will be destroyed is this earth. The Lord, in speaking to Satan, said: "Therefore will I bring forth a fire from the midst of thee, it shall devour thee, and I will bring thee to ashes upon the earth in the sight of all them that behold thee." [Ezek. 28:18] God will have a clean universe, because both sin and sinner will be destroyed. "For evildoers shall be cut off: but those that wait upon the Lord, they shall inherit the earth. For yet a little while, and the wicked shall not be: yea, thou shalt diligently consider his place, and it shall not be.... But the wicked shall perish, and the enemies of the Lord shall be as the fat of lambs: they shall consume; into smoke shall they consume away." [Ps. 37: 9, 10, 20]

The Greek verb *tartaroō* means to cast into the lower regions, into which the devil was cast after his rebellion in heaven. He has been cast out into this earth, where he dwells in an atmosphere of spiritual darkness, being shut out from the light of God. The apostle John says that "the great dragon was cast out, that old serpent, called the Devil, and Satan, which deceiveth the whole world: he was cast into the earth, and his angels were cast out with him." [Rev. 12:9] This planet is the place where Satan is confined since his expulsion from heaven. "God spared not the angels that sinned, but cast them down to hell [*tartaroō*], and delivered them into chains of darkness, to be reserved unto judgment." [2 Pet. 2:4]

"Reserved unto judgment." How can one accuse God of punishing sinners before He judges them? "The Lord knoweth how to deliver the godly out of temptations, and to reserve the unjust unto the day of judgment to be punished." [2 Pet. 2:9] The apostle Peter also declares that "the heavens and the earth, which are now, by the same word are kept in store, reserved unto fire against the day of judgment and perdition of ungodly men....But the day of the Lord will come as a thief in the night; in the which the heavens shall pass away with a great noise, and the elements shall melt with fervent heat, the earth also and the works that are therein shall be burned up." [2 Pet. 3:7, 10]

In summing up the evidence from the Scriptures of truth on this important subject, it is clear that (a) there is no such place as a Gehenna existing now; (b) that the deceased sinner is sleeping in the grave, awaiting the resurrection day, at which time he will receive the "wages of sin" — eternal death; (e) that the punishment for sin will be administered by means of devouring fire; (d) that as the result of this burning the wicked will be reduced to ashes; (e) that it will be on this earth that the final destruction of both Satan and unrepentant sinners will take place; (f) that when the earth shall have been purged by fire, there will be a new earth.

Eternal Torment in Hell

The doctrine of a present-burning hell where the wicked are plunged at death, there to burn through the rounds of eternity, has given men a distorted and incorrect conception of the character of our blessed Lord and His Christ. How the heart of Satan has pulsated with joy on hearing both priests and ministers of the church vividly portraying to their congregations the imagined condition of the writhing victims in that flaming abyss!

After listening to such a terrible description of the fate of sinners, who would not arrive at the conclusion that the Creator of the universe is anything but the pitying friend of sinners? Trembling faith would not dare reach up to heaven and claim pardon of such a stern and inexorable God. In all such base and fabricated teaching, the father of lies delights.

While we have a God who hates sin, yet He loves the sinner beyond anything that the human mind can comprehend. He will leave nothing undone to save those who in humility and faith will come to Him for pardon and grace. An unregenerated person may listen to the preaching of hell fire until doom's day, but' all the roaring flames of Dante's *Inferno* will never lead that individual to Jesus Christ. It is love, and not fear, that converts a soul. One glimpse into that benignant face of the loving Saviour hanging upon the cross, dying such an ignominious death for poor fallen humanity, can melt the hard heart and cause doubt and fear to be dispelled. A repelling hatred for sin and all that it entails will enter the human breast when the love of God is comprehended. The only remedy for the fear-tormented minds that have imbibed the fictitious and speculative doctrine of a present-burning hell is to study the Holy Scriptures and bask in the presence of Christ's divine love. Those who have experienced this can attest to the truthfulness of the statement written by the beloved apostle: "There is no fear in love; but perfect love casteth out fear: because fear hath torment. He that feareth is not

The Wine of Roman Babylon

made perfect in love. We love Him, because He first loved us." [1 John 4:18, 19]

Also see the Appendix p. 225.

CHAPTER XV

Extreme Unction

THE FOURTEENTH sip from the Babylonian cup is "Extreme Unction." The teaching and belief in the efficacy of this ceremony is greatly cherished by every devout Roman Catholic. To be deprived of the graces supposed to remove both venial and mortal sins is considered a tragedy not only for the deceased but also for those who are left to mourn. The person who dies without having had the administration of the sacrament of extreme unction by a priest is looked upon as being unprepared for death.

Asks one questioner: "Q. If his sickness be mortal, what should he wish for more earnestly than to die happy, which this holy sacrament gives him grace to do?" The reply given is thus: "A. Relatives also, or attendants, of the sick person, sin grievously, if through their fault the last sacraments are not administered to him in due time."[113]

This sacrament of the Roman Catholic Church is described in the following statements:

> "Extreme unction is the sacrament that gives spiritual strength and bodily comfort to those who are in danger of death by sickness. The grace of this sacrament is given by the anointing with holy oil and the prayer of the priest. This sacrament is called extreme unction, because it is the last of the holy unctions which are administered by the [Roman] Church. The Council of Trent declares: 'If any one assert that extreme unction is not really and truly a sacrament

---
113   Deharbe, 300.

instituted by Christ our Lord, and described by St. James the apostle, but that it is only a rite adopted by the fathers, or a human invention, let him be anathema.'—Session XIV, Canon I. The Holy Scriptures teach: 'Is any man sick among you? Let him bring in the priests of the [Roman] Church, and let them pray over him, anointing him with oil in the name of the Lord. And the prayer of faith shall save the sick man; and the Lord shall raise him up; and if he be in sins, they shall be forgiven him.'—St. James, Chapter V, verses 14, 15. Extreme unction increases sanctifying grace and remits venial sin. In some extraordinary cases it can also remit mortal sin. It likewise removes the remains of sin, by which we mean the inclination to evil and the weakness of will which are the result of our sins, and which remain after our sins have been forgiven."[114]

"Q. What is extreme unction? A. Extreme unction is a sacrament which gives grace to those who are in danger of death from sickness or injury. Q. What does extreme unction do fur the soul? A. Extreme unction cleanses the soul from the remains of sin and strengthens it against the power of Satan. Q. How does extreme unction cleanse the soul from the remains of sin? A. Extreme unction remits venial sins and those mortal sins which the sick person can no longer confess and takes away the evil effects of sin."[115]

Extreme unction, which is the last rite of the Roman Church, is one of the most delicate and solemn questions to handle. These quotations taken from the catechisms clearly indicate that this sacrament is administered for the purpose of preparing the individual for death. The devil will work with all his power to keep a person, while he is in good health, from confessing his sins and laying hold of the grace of Christ to enable him to keep from sinning. If Satan can keep a person bound by the cords of his sins and dependent on this papal sacrament of extreme unction, as a last-moment means of liquidating a life of sin, he has accomplished his object. The claim is made that this

---

[114] Butler, 275.
[115] MacEachen, 131, 132.

Extreme Unction

sacrament has such sanctifying grace that the priests in administering it have the power to remit even mortal sins.

Extreme unction may be properly called the sacrament of the dying, because only those who are nearing the portals of the grave are permitted to receive it. In a canon of the Council of Trent it was specifically declared that extreme unction should be administered only to those dangerously ill. Note the following:

> "They must be sick, as St. James declares, and the Council of Trent understands the apostle to speak of dangerous sickness. Hence the sacrament is not intended for persons ill but not dangerously ill, or, again, for such as are in danger of death but not from sickness."[116]

> "Q. What is meant by the last sacrament? A. Confession, holy communion and extreme unction are called the last sacraments when given to the dying."[117]

Although the Roman Catholic Church claims, in administration of the sacrament of extreme unction, to follow out the instruction laid down in James 5: 14, 15, it will be seen that there is a vast difference between the simplicity of the teaching of Holy Writ and the papal ceremony. Let us note a few contrasting features. It was voted in the Decree of Union at the Council of Florence that the oil was to be applied to different parts of the body when administering the sacrament of extreme unction.

> "The Council of Florence, in the Decree of Union, prescribes that the unction is to be given with olive oil on eyes, ears, nostrils, mouth, hands, feet, and reins, and such is the present custom of the [Roman] Church, except that the *unctio renum* is omitted in the case of women. Some theologians hold that without unction of the five senses the sacrament is invalid....According to the Roman ritual the oil is applied in the form of a cross."[118]

---

[116] Wm. E. Addis and Thomas Arnold, "Extreme Unction," *A Catholic Dictionary*, 333, 334.
[117] MacEachen, 132.
[118] Wm. E. Addis and Thomas Arnold, ibid.

The Wine of Roman Babylon

One may search the New Testament from Matthew to Revelation and not find one intimation of the application of the oil to the various senses or the parts of the body. How could the Council of Florence, held in 1438-1442, legislate in regard to the application of the oil when the word of God is silent on it? The Holy Bible does not specify what kind of oil should be used, neither does it state that the oil must be blessed by the bishop, nor that it should be applied in any particular manner. We are told:

> "Since the seventh century the holy oils, formerly consecrated at any time, have been blessed by the bishop in the mass of this day. Twelve priests and seven deacons assist as witnesses of the ceremony. The bishop and priests breathe three times upon the oil of the catechumens and the chrism-, meaning by this action that the power of the Holy Spirit is about to descend on the oils; and after the consecration is complete they salute the oils with the words, 'Hail, holy oil; hail, holy chrism.'"[119]

The oil which is now used by the Roman Church is consecrated on the so-called Holy Thursday of Passion Week, the week before Easter. Before the seventh century the oil was consecrated at any time, but now it is blessed by the bishop on this one occasion.

The scriptural injunction calls for "the elders," a plurality of administrators. "Is any sick among you? Let him call for the elders of the church; and let them pray over him, anointing him with oil in the name of the Lord." [James 5:14] On the other hand, the Roman Catholic Church requires but one administrator, a priest. "The priest is the minister of extreme unction."[120]

The simplicity of the apostolic anointing is in marked contrast to the display and complicated ceremony carried out by the Catholic priests. Here is the way they do it:

---

119 Ibid., "Holy Week," 404, 405.
120 Geiermann, 87.

Extreme Unction

"Q. What Should be provided in the sick room? A. In the sick room there should be provided a table or stand with a white cover. On it should be placed a crucifix, two wax candies, holy water, a glass of drinking water and a teaspoon. Q. What should those about the house do when the priest arrives? A. When the priest arrives, those about the house should instantly fall on their knees to adore the blessed sacrament which he carries on his bosom."[121]

One may look in vain in the Sacred Scriptures to find such an outline of furnishings to be provided before the sick can be anointed. The Roman Catholic Church truly has drifted a long way from the original ceremony of anointing the sick.

The twelve disciples whom Jesus sent forth to preach the gospel "anointed with oil many that were sick." [Mark 6:13] But the Bible does not say that the people they anointed were near death. The purpose of the anointing by the disciples was for the healing of the sick and for their restoration to health. Contrary to the original plan, designed by God, the Roman Church administers its extreme unction as a means of granting forgiveness of sins and of conveying tile graces of God to the soul as the final preparation for death. The Holy Scriptures set forth the anointing as for healing and life and not for death: "Is any sick among you? Let him call for the elders of the church; and let them pray over him, anointing him with oil in the name of the Lord: and the prayer of faith shall save the sick, and the Lord shall raise him up; and if he have committed sins, they shall be forgiven him." [James 5:14, 15]

The wording of the apostolic instruction is so simple and explicit that no one need doubt that the anointing spoken of is for life and not for death. The person who is ill and desires to follow the instruction laid down by the apostle James must believe that God will do what the Sacred Tome says He will; that is, that He "shall raise him

---
121 MacEachen, 134.

The Wine of Roman Babylon

up" from his bed of sickness. In contrast to this, the Roman Catholic who calls for the priest to administer the rite of extreme unction does so in anticipation of death, in order to effect a happy demise. So says a writer of the papal church:

"Of the effect of extreme unction the Council of Trent says: 'This effect is the grace of the Holy Ghost whose unction blots out sins, if any remain to be expiated, and the consequences of sins; and alleviates and strengthens the soul of the sick person by exciting in him a great confidence in the divine mercy, sustained by which he bears more lightly the troubles and sufferings of disease, and more easily resists the temptations of the demon waiting for his heel; and sometimes, when it is expedient for the soul's salvation, recovers bodily health.'"[122]

"The effects of extreme unction are: (1) an increase of grace; (2) resignation to God's will; (3) comfort in pain; (4) strength in temptation; (5) remission of venial sin; (6) remission of mortal sins, if the sick person be sorry for them; (7) the restoration of health if God see fit."[123]

This rite, as taught by the Roman Church, points the soul, in the last moments of life, not to the loving Saviour, who alone is the resurrection and the life, but to the human agent and also to reliance upon an outward ceremony to prepare one for death. As we compare the scriptural outline of the simple service of anointing with oil for the restoration of the body with the ritualistic procedure involved in the papal sacrament of extreme unction, how grateful we should be for the beauty and simplicity of the gospel which provides healing for both the soul and the body!

Never shall I forget the experience we had in my, home in the last illness of my father. A priest was called to administer the last rite to him. The table with the crucifix, the wax candles, the holy water, the glass of water, and the teaspoon were made ready. It was a sad time for the

---
[122] Martin, 277.
[123] Geiermann, 86.

Extreme Unction

family, as its head was slowly approaching death. On such occasions, when the priest enters the home carrying the "holy viaticum," all are required to bow in adoration. Knowing what the Sacred Scriptures teach on this subject, I left the room where my family were, because I could neither countenance nor be a party to such idolatry as was there displayed.

If extreme unction did for my father all that "The Convert's Catechism" claims it does, namely, effect the "remission of venial sin" and the "remission of mortal sin," then why did my family have masses said for him after his decease? If the priests truly believe in the administration of this rite and their far-reaching claims for it, why do they continue to offer masses for those who have been the recipients of extreme unction? Such uncertainties give little consolation to either the dying or those who are left to mourn.

This doctrine of extreme unction is not founded on the eternal truths of the written word of God. Therefore, cease to linger by the cup whose enchantment leads away from the simple instruction laid down by the Lord.

Also see the Appendix p. 227.

The Wine of Roman Babylon

CHAPTER XVI

Sunday Observance

OF ALL the draughts taken from the intoxicating cup of Babylon none is more widely accepted than "Sunday Observance." The question of Sunday observance has resulted in much discussion among theologians. However, on this vital point there should be no conflict of opinion, because the Sacred Bible and the Roman Catholic Church by their decided testimonies leave no room for doubt or conjecturing as to the introduction of the observance of the first day of the week among Christians. That the seventh-day Sabbath is ordained by the fourth commandment of the Decalogue, is not only supported by the word of God, but is generally admitted by professing Christians.

The true Sabbath — the seventh day — is a divine institution which the beneficent Creator has passed down to us from the Carden of Eden. "Thus the heavens and the earth were finished, and all the host of them. And on the seventh day God ended His work which He had made; and He rested on the seventh day from all His work which He had made. And God blessed the seventh day, and sanctified it: because that in it He had rested from all His work which God created and made." [Gen. 2:1-3]

The inspired account of the institution of the Sabbath reveals the following: (1) that the creation was a completed or finished work; (2) that God rested, not as one weary or fatigued, but with perfect satisfaction in the completion of His handiwork; (3) that He put His blessing on the seventh

The Wine of Roman Babylon

day; and (4) that He sanctified—set apart for holy use the seventh day. It still remains a holy day even to the present time. "For Thou blessest, O Lord, and it shall be blessed forever." [1 Chron. 17:27] The divine benediction which made the seventh day, the Sabbath, a holy day has never been withdrawn. After resting upon the seventh day and placing His blessing on it, the Lord sanctified it, and set it apart as a holy rest day for man to observe. God designed that in the keeping of the Sabbath man should regard Him as the Creator and Sovereign of this earth. The Sabbath institution is, therefore, the memorial which God gave to remind man of the birth of this world. Those who recognize it as such will give the Lord His rightful place as ruler not only of the vast universe, but also of the human heart, because the Sabbath is a memorial, or sign, of redemption as well as of creation.

Adam and his posterity knew which day of the week was the Sabbath day. The Sabbath was never lost sight of down through the ages, for there were always those who remained true to the divine command and would rather die than violate God's holy precept. When His people were brought out of Egypt, the Lord gave them a constant reminder of the definite seventh day and of its sacredness by working a threefold miracle every week for forty years. This He did (1) by raining down a double quantity of manna on the sixth day of the week; (2) by preserving the food so it would keep over the Sabbath, which miraculous preservation never occurred on any other day of the week; and (3) by locking the heavens so that no manna fell on the seventh day. [Exod. 16:4, 5, 18–30] Therefore, the sacred obligation of the Sabbath institution was kept constantly before the people of God during their sojourn in the wilderness. On entering the promised land they brought with them the Sabbath, and thus the identical seventh day has been preserved to the present. "And [He] gave them the lands of the heathen: and they inherited the labor of the people; that they might observe His statutes, and keep His laws. Praise ye the Lord." [Ps. 105:44, 45]

It was during the wilderness experience that the Lord, escorted by a retinue of angels, came down upon Mount Sinai and declared by an audible voice the Ten Commandments, the center of which is the seventh-day Sabbath. The people who heard the peals of thunder, saw the lightning flash, felt the old earth tremble beneath their feet, and heard the voice of the Mighty One of heaven proclaiming His Sabbath, were not to forget this precept, nor lightly esteem its binding claims. They could be in no doubt as to which day of the week God recognized as His. "Thou camest down also upon Mount Sinai, and spakest with them from heaven, and gavest them right judgments, and true laws, good statutes and commandments: and madest known unto them Thy holy Sabbath." [Neh. 9:13, 14]

Jesus Christ, during the thirty-three and a half years of His life on this earth, observed the seventh day. Thus by precept and example He demonstrated its binding claims upon the life of His followers. "And He came to Nazareth, where He had been brought up: and, as His custom was, He went into the synagogue on the Sabbath day, and stood up for to read." [Luke 4:16]

It is by the observance of the true Sabbath—the seventh day—that the Christian commemorates the creative and recreative power of God. "Moreover also I gave them My Sabbaths, to be a sign between Me and them, that they might know that I am the Lord that sanctify them.... And hallow My Sabbaths; and they shall be a sign between Me and you, that ye may know that I am the Lord your God." [Ezek. 20:12, 20]

The footsteps of the Son of God lead to the keeping, of the day which the commandment specifies. The unchangeableness and immutability of the law of God have been vindicated by Christ through His strict adherence to every one of its precepts, and also by His sacrifice on the cross. If Christ abolished God's law and abrogated the seventh-day Sabbath at the cross, as some claim, He thus would be giving license to people to break any or all of the Ten Commandments.

"The Lord is well pleased for His righteousness' sake; He will magnify the law, and make it honorable." [Isa. 42:21] The greatest honor Christ could confer upon the law was His own conformity to every principle of the Ten Commandments. He, the greatest teacher who ever lived, made the Decalogue the embodiment of His teachings. In the Sermon on the Mount, the Ten Commandments are the burden of His message. "Think not that I am come to destroy the law, or the prophets: I am not come to destroy, but to fulfill. For verily I say unto you, Till heaven and earth pass, one jot or one tittle shall in no wise pass from the law, till all be fulfilled." [Matt. 5:17, 18] "And it is easier for heaven and earth to pass, than one tittle of the law to fail. [Luke 16:17] Our Saviour did not destroy the law, but by His death He established it, and our faith in His atoning blood will establish our confidence in its unalterable, and holy character. "Do we then make void the law through faith? God forbid: yea, we establish the law." [Rom. 3:31]

Again, in the death of the Son of God we have the Sabbath of the fourth commandment brought vividly to light. Knowing what would be the results of the sacrifice which He was making, and being fully aware of its completion, the Saviour cried, "It is finished." [John 19:30] Joseph's new tomb was ready, and the Son of God was laid peacefully to rest as the holy Sabbath approached. The One who indited the words "Thus the heavens and the earth were finished," [Gen. 2:1] at the close of creation week and commemorated the event by resting on the seventh day, is the One who, while on the cross, exclaimed: "It is finished," [John 19:30] thus recognizing the consummation and accomplishment of the work of redemption, or re-creation. The Sabbath of creation, the day on which Christ rested in the grave, was still to be observed to commemorate both creation and redemption.

"This man [Joseph of Arimathaea] went unto Pilate, and begged the body of Jesus. And he took it down, and wrapped it in linen, and laid it in a sepulcher that was hewn in stone, wherein never man before was laid. And that day was the preparation, and the Sabbath drew on. And the women also, which came with Him from Galilee, followed after, and beheld the sepulcher, and how His body was laid. And they returned, and prepared spices and ointments; and *rested the Sabbath day according to the commandment.*" [Luke 23:52-56]

If Christ had intimated that the Sabbath was transferred to the first day of the week, the Christian women mentioned in Holy Scripture as attending His burial knew nothing about it, for "they rested the Sabbath day according to the commandment," and would not anoint the body of their Lord on the seventh day. However, on the first day of the week, when they wended their way to the sepulcher to perform that which they would not do on the Sabbath, they found their Lord had risen. He, too, had rested on the seventh day, and did not break the portals of the tomb until the sacred hours of the Sabbath had passed. "And when the Sabbath was past, Mary Magdalene, and Mary the mother of James, and Salome, had bought sweet spices, that they might come and anoint him. And very early in the morning the first day of the week, they came unto the sepulcher at the rising of the sun." [Mark 16:1, 2]

Christ's coming forth from the dead on the first day of the week does not make it a sacred day any more than His dying on Friday made the sixth day holy. If the Sabbath instituted at creation, and kept by our Lord and His followers, had been repealed by a command of Christ, it certainly would have been recorded in the Holy Scriptures. If the change of the Sabbath was to be one of "the things which must shortly come to pass," [Rev. 1:1] John would have mentioned it in the Book of Revelation. But one may search the New Testament from Matthew to Jude and not find any command to keep the first day instead of the seventh. The Book of Revelation, which closes the inspired canon, is strangely silent on the matter. If Christ had intended that the Sabbath of creation should be set aside, He never would have commanded His disciples to pray for nearly forty years that their flight from Jerusalem should not be on the Sabbath day. [Matt. 24:20] This shows that the Sabbath was to be kept by Christians from the time this precept was given until A.D. 70, when Jerusalem was destroyed by the Roman army.

Is it not strange that Sunday is almost universally observed when the Sacred Writings do not indorse it? Satan, the great counterfeiter, worked through the "mystery of iniquity" to introduce a counterfeit Sabbath to take the place of the true Sabbath of Jehovah. Sunday stands side by side with Ash Wednesday, Palm Sunday, Holy (or Maundy) Thursday, Good Friday, Easter Sunday, Whitsunday, Corpus Christi, Assumption Day, All Souls' Day, Christmas Day, and a host of other ecclesiastical feast days too numerous to mention. This array of Roman Catholic feasts. and fast days are all man made. None of them bears the divine credentials of the Author of the Inspired Word.

There is nothing more reassuring to the earnest seeker for truth than to find described in the "sure word of prophecy" [2 Pet. 1:19] the power which would be guilty of attempting to change God's holy law. "And be shall. speak great words against the Most High, and shall wear out the saints of the Most High, and think to change times and laws: and they shall be given into his hand until a time and times and the dividing of time." [Dan. 7:25] This prophecy applies with overwhelming force to a religious system

Sunday Observance

which would "speak great words against the Most High." The Holy Bible, world history, and theologians themselves, make it so evident who is referred to by the prophecy, that anyone can readily see what power it foretold. The "man of sin," about whom Paul wrote [2 Thess. 2:3–7], had been mentioned over five hundred years before by the prophet Daniel. The apostle foretold something of the blasphemous claims of the one who would exalt himself above God, who would not blush in declaring himself to be the "Vicar of Christ," and would assume nearly every name and title that have been attributed to the Godhead. Says one papal prelate:

> "All the names which in the Scriptures are applied to Christ, by virtue of which it is established that He is over the church, all the same names are applied to the pope."[124]

He would "wear out the saints of the Most High." During the Dark Ages God's people suffered under the scrutiny of the eyes of this religious, persecuting power. Intrigues, plots, and schemes designed to vex and harass the poor "heretic" were used to exterminate those who opposed the doctrines propounded by the apostate church. The rack, the fagot, and the other tortures used by the Inquisition took their toll. Historians number these slain by religious persecution as being between 50,000,000 and 75,000,000. Some say the total was more. Roman Catholic leaders admit this:

> "During the 2,000 years the [Roman] Church has been on this earth, she has warred with nearly every government in this world. The world is full of their ruins. Their thrones have toppled over and fallen, their dynasties have come to dust. And the governments of the world today will meet the same fate if they challenge the hostility of the church of God. She remains; she is today what she was 2,000 years ago; she

---

[124] Robert Cardinal Bellarmine, *"De Conciliorum Auctoritate"* (On the Authority of the Councils), Bk. 2, chap. 17, *Disputationes de Controversiis Christianae Fidei adversus Hujus Temporis Haereticos*, v2 (Venice: J. Malachinus, 1721) 47, col. 2.

is today what she was in the days of Justinian the Great; she is today what she was in the days of Barbarossa; she is today what she was during the Middle Ages; she is today what she was during the times of Protestant persecution, during and since the sixteenth century; she is the invincible church of God. God help the state that attacks her; God help the king that provokes her hostility."[125]

A papal periodical has said with boasting:

"The [Roman] Church has persecuted. Only a tyro in church history will deny that. The apologists in the days of Roman imperial domination inveighed against persecution, and with Tertullian declared that it was no part of religion to persecute religion. But after the days of Constantine, and under the reign of that first Christian emperor, the attitude of Christians underwent a change, and persecution of pagans took place in many places in the empire. One hundred fifty years after Constantine the Donatists were persecuted, and sometimes put to death. Against this extreme measure St. Augustine raised his voice; but he was willing that they should be despoiled of their churches and of their goods. Protestants were persecuted in France and Spain with the full approval of the [Roman] Church authorities. We have always defended the persecution of the Huguenots, and the Spanish inquisition. Wherever and whenever there is honest [Roman] Catholicity, there will be a clear distinction drawn between truth and error, and [Roman] Catholicity and all forms of heresy. When she thinks it good to use physical force, she will use it. But will the [Roman] Catholic Church give bond that she will not persecute at all? Will she guarantee absolute freedom and equality of all churches and all faiths? The (Roman] Catholic Church gives no bonds for her good behavior....She has countenanced violence when more humane measures would have been of more avail. Her children and her clergy

---

[125] Extract from a sermon preached by D. S. Phelan on Sunday, December 12, 1909, and published in *The Western Watchman*, a Roman Catholic periodical, December 16, 1909.

Sunday Observance

have often been carried away by popular passion. But she gives no bonds that such things shall not occur again."[126]

Another writer tells the story succinctly in these words, which give significant statistics on tile various persecutions endured by the followers of Christ:

"From the birth of popery in 606, to the present time, it is estimated by careful and credible historians, that more than 50,000,000 of the human family, have been slaughtered for the crime of heresy by popish persecutors, an average of more than *40,000 religious murders* for every year of the existence of popery. Of course the average number of victims yearly, was vastly greater, during the gloomy ages when popery was in her glory and reigned Despot of the World; and it has been much less since the power of the popes has diminished to tyrannize over the nations, and to compel the princes of the earth, by the terrors of excommunication, interdiction, and deposition, to butcher their heretical subjects."[127]

"An 100,000 Albigenses fell, it is said, in one day: and their bodies were heaped together and burned. Detachments of soldiery were, for three months, despatched in every direction to demolish houses, destroy vineyards, and ruin the hopes of the husbandman. The females were defiled. The march of the *holy warriors* was marked by the flames of burning houses, the screams of violated women, and the groans of murdered men. The war, with all its sanguinary accompaniments, lasted 20 years, and the Albigenses, during this time, were not the only sufferers. Three hundred thousand crusaders fell on the plains of Languedoc, and fattened the soil with their blood.

"All this barbarity was perpetrated in the name of religion. The carnage was celebrated as the triumph of the church, the honour of the papacy, and the glory of [Roman] Catholicism. The pope proclaimed the *holy war* in the name of the Lord. The army of the cross exulted in the massacre of Lavaur, and the clergy sung a hymn to the Creator for the

---

126 *The Western Watchman* (Dec 24, 1908).
127 Dowling, 541,542.

The Wine of Roman Babylon

glorious victory. The assassins thanked the God of mercy for the work of destruction and bloodshed. The soldiery, in the morning, attended high mass, and then proceeded, during the day, to waste the country and murder its population. The assassination of 60,000 citizens of Beziers was accounted, says Mariana, 'the visible judgment of heaven.' According to Benedict, 'the heresy of Albigensianism drew down the wrath of God on the country of Languedoc.'"[128]

The Roman Catholic Church admits that she put numbers to death who refused to bow to her mandates. The blood of countless martyrs has been crying to God for justice down through the stream of time, and it may seem to an incredulous world that He has forgotten the crimes of Babylon. But Jesus has said: "And shall not God avenge His own elect, which cry day and night unto Him, though He bear long with them?" [Luke 18:7] The poet well says:

> *"Careless seems the great Avenger; history's pages but record*
>
> *One death-grapple in the darkness 'twixt old systems and the Word;*
>
> *Truth forever on the scaffold, wrong forever on the throne, –*
>
> *Yet that scaffold sways the future, and, behind the dim unknown,*
>
> *Standeth God within the shadow, keeping watch above His own."*[129]

"He shall think to change the times and the law." [Dan. 7:25] Has Rome thought to change the law of God? Let her own works testify to the indictment:

> "You may read the Bible from Genesis to Revelation, and you will not find a single line authorizing the sanctification of Sunday. The Scriptures enforce the religious observance of Saturday, a day which we never sanctify."[130]

---

128   Edgar, 257, 258.
129   James Russell Lowell, "The Present Crisis," *in The Poetical Works of James Russell Lowell*, household ed. (Boston: Houghton Mifflin Co., 1916) 6.
130   Gibbons, 89.

Sunday Observance

"Q. Have you any other way of proving that the [Roman] Church has power to institute festivals of precept? A. Had she not such power, she could not have done that in which all modern religionists agree with her; — she could not have substituted the observance of Sunday the first day of the week, for the observance of Saturday the seventh day, a change for which there is no Scriptural authority."[131]

"The [Roman] Catholic Church for over 1,000 years before the existence of a Protestant, by virtue of her divine mission, changed the day from Saturday to Sunday....The Christian Sabbath is therefore *to this day* the acknowledged offspring of the [Roman] Catholic Church, as spouse of the Holy Ghost, without a word of remonstrance from the Protestant world."[132]

"Q. Which is the Sabbath day? A. Saturday is the Sabbath day. Q. Why do we observe Sunday instead of Saturday? A. We observe Sunday instead of Saturday because the [Roman] Catholic Church, in the Council of Laodicea (A. D. 336), transferred the solemnity from Saturday to Sunday."[133]

"Some of the truths that have been handed down to us by tradition and are not recorded in the Sacred Scripture, are the following: that there are just seven sacraments; that there is a purgatory; that, in the new law, Sunday should be kept holy instead of the Sabbath; that infants should be baptized, and that there are precisely seventy-two books in the Bible."[134]

"Q. When Protestants do profane work upon Saturday, or the seventh day of the week, do they follow the Scripture as their only rule of faith, — do they find this permission clearly laid down in the Sacred Volume? A . On the contrary, they have only the authority of tradition for this practice. In profaning Saturday, they violate one of God's commandments, which He has never clearly abrogated, — 'Remember thou keep holy the Sabbath day.' Q. Is the observance of Sunday, as the day of rest, a matter clearly laid down in

---

[131] Stephen Keenan, *A Doctrinal Catechism* (New York: P. J. Kenedy & Sons) 174.
[132] *The Catholic Mirror* (Sept. 23, 1893).
[133] Geiermann, 50.
[134] Butler, 63.

The Wine of Roman Babylon

Scripture? A. It certainly is not; and yet all Protestants consider the observance of this particular day as essentially necessary to salvation. To say, we observe the Sunday, because Christ rose from the dead on that day, is to say we act without warrant of Scripture; and we might as well say that we should rest on Thursday because Christ ascended to heaven on that day, and rested in reality from the work of redemption."[135]

"Q. What do we conclude from all this? A. That Protestants have no Scripture for the measure of their day of rest, that they abolish the observance of Saturday without warrant of Scripture,—that they substitute Sunday in its place without Scriptural authority,—consequently, that for all this, they have only traditional authority. Yet Protestants would look upon a man who would do profane work after five o'clock on Sunday, or keep the Saturday and profane the first day, as a victim of perdition. Hence we must conclude, that the Scripture, which does not teach these things clearly, does not contain all necessary truths, and, consequently, cannot be the only rule of faith."[136]

"It was the [Roman] Catholic Church which, by the authority of Jesus Christ, has transferred this rest to the Sunday in remembrance of the resurrection of our Lord. Thus the observance of Sunday by the Protestants is an homage they pay, in spite of themselves, to the authority of the [Roman) Church."[137]

"We [Roman] Catholics, then, have precisely the same authority for keeping Sunday holy instead of Saturday as we have for every other article of our creed; namely, the authority of 'the church of the living God, the pillar and ground of the truth' (1 Tim. 3: 15); whereas you who are Protestants have really no authority for it whatever; for there is no authority for it in the Bible, and you will not allow that there can be authority for it anywhere else. Both you and we do, in fact, follow tradition in this matter; but we follow it,

---

[135] Keenan, 352, 354–355.
[136] Ibid.
[137] Mgr. Segur, *Plain Talk about the Protestantism of Today* (Boston: T. B. Noonan & Co., 1868) 213.

Sunday Observance

believing it to be a part of God's word, and the [Roman] Church to be its divinely appointed guardian and interpreter; you follow it, denouncing it all the time as a fallible and treacherous guide, which often 'makes the commandment of God of none effect.'"[138]

By attempting to change God's holy law this religious system really tries to exalt itself above Him. If any one knowingly and understandingly observes Sunday as a religious day, he obeys and gives homage to that power which claims to have made the change. Consequently allegiance is rendered to the pope rather than to God. The apostles of Christ say: "We ought to obey God rather than men." [Acts 5:29] This divinely inspired counsel is still good.

While Sunday has been accepted and observed by many, yet God has those today who observe the true Sabbath, the seventh day. Seventh-day Adventists, loyal to Christ and God's law, constitute the true church today, Their work of reform was foretold by Isaiah: "Cry aloud, spare not, lift up thy voice like a trumpet, and show My people their transgression, and the house of Jacob their sins....And they that shall be of thee shall build the old waste places: thou shalt raise up the foundations of many generations; and thou shalt be called, The repairer of the breach, The restorer of paths to dwell in. If thou turn away thy foot from the Sabbath, from doing thy pleasure on My holy day; and call the Sabbath a delight, the holy of the Lord, honorable; and shalt honor Him, not doing thine own ways, nor finding thine own pleasure, nor speaking thine own words: then shalt thou delight thyself in the Lord; and I will cause thee to ride upon the high places of the earth, and feed

---

[138] The Brotherhood of St. Paul, "Why Don't You Keep Holy the Sabbath Day? – A question for All Bible Christians," in *The Clifton Tracts* (Library of Controversy), v4, tract 4 (New York: P. J. Kenedy) 15.

thee with the heritage of Jacob thy father: for the mouth of the Lord hath spoken it." [Isa. 58: 1, 12-14]

The message concerning the Sabbath is being heralded around the world. The divine institution hallowed by the Creator will be accepted by those who make the Sacred Scriptures their guide. Those who willingly accept the papal institution which rests on human tradition and the authority of the apostate church will suffer the inevitable result. God will never permit any willful transgressor of His law to enter heaven. [Matt. 7:21-23; Heb. 10:26; Rev. 22:14, 15] Historical facts, Scriptural evidence, and papal admissions tell the inquirers for truth that they are without excuse if they refuse to keep the true Sabbath of the Lord.

It is the external attractiveness of the church represented by the fallen woman of the prophecy [Rev. 17], with her imposing ceremonies and seductive influence, that leads unwary feet to the delusive cup to sip of the wine of her false doctrines. Multitudes find the contents of this cup more palatable to their carnal desires than they do the pure water of life which the word of God offers.

There is nothing that God desires so much as obedience to His word. [1 Sam. 15:16-23; John 15:10, 14; 1 John 2:3-5; 3:22; 5:2, 3] While many may steel their hearts and shut their eyes against the truth, yet some from all the various churches, Roman Catholic and Protestant alike, are responding to the call of heaven. They will follow the Holy Bible, and the Bible alone, as their guide. Like Paul of old, they will inquire, "Lord, what wilt Thou have me to do?" [Acts 9:6] Blessed is the man or the woman who has to suffer for his Lord. [Matt. 5:10-12] Heaven with all its glories will be cheap enough regardless of the price. [2 Cor. 4:17] When the last day shall come, and Christ shall separate the inhabitants of this world into two classes, it will matter little where proud pontiffs, richly robed cardinals, and learned divines with their scholastic philosophy may stand. What will concern each of us most will be: Where is my blessed Saviour? On which side is He? His banner with this inscription will be waving over His people: "Here is the patience of the saints: here are they that keep the commandments of God, and the faith of Jesus." [Rev. 14:12] And He will say: "Blessed are they that do His commandments, that they may have right to the tree of life, and may enter in through the gates into the city." [Rev. 22:14]

Also see the Appendix p. 229.

APPENDICES

The Wine of Roman Babylon

Appendix to Chapter I

Two Systems of Worship

From the days of Cain and Abel there have been two systems of worship—the true and the false. The Scriptures have drawn a distinct line between the genuine and the counterfeit. "I am the Lord, and there is none else, there is no God beside me." (Isa.45:5)

Paganism originated with Nimrod and his contemporaries, over two thousand years before Christ. Its corrupt and idolatrous teaching spread so rapidly that its dark pall seemed to have enveloped, blinded and debased to a large extent the whole human race. Satan, the enemy of truth, set up a form of religious worship to pervert the true gospel of Jesus Christ. Through paganism the counterfeit of the gospel was established and has continued even to the present.

A study of the beliefs and rituals of Brahmanism, Buddhism, Zoroastrianism and all other heathen religions will attest to the fact that paganism has and is being perpetuated. The greater portion of earth's inhabitants are worshipers of the mystic and pagan deities of ancient Babylon. So powerful has been the influence of the Babylonian or pagan doctrines that only a small segment of the human family are worshipers of the true God.

What has given this false system of religion its marvelous vitality and potency to be able to resist the divine power and teachings of the Holy Bible? The answer can be given unequivocally. It is Satan, the enemy of God and His truth. He is responsible for the multiplicity of the religious persuasions that have brought nothing but confusion among Christians. If all who claim to believe the Bible and what it teaches were to follow explicitly its divine instruction, there would be but one church. What a bulwark it would be against all heathen religions!

While Satan has been busily engaged in propagating his false doctrines through the "Babylonian Mysteries," God has not been silent. He, through His prophets, has given ample warning against the counterfeit doctrines and false worship so freely believed and practiced. Let us examine some texts from God's Word bearing on this subject. "To the law and to the testimony: if they speak not according to this word, it is because there is no light in them." (Isa. 8:20) The first and second commandments of the Decalogue imperatively forbid the worship of any god but Jehovah (Exod. 20:3-6). He adds this injunction: "Make no mention of the name of other gods, neither let it be heard out of thy mouth." (Exod. 23:13—see also Deut. 4:15-19)

The admonition of the Lord was given to Jeremiah in these words: "Thus saith the Lord, learn not the way of the heathen." (Jer. 10:2) "The way of the heathen" means the idolatry of the heathen. It embraces and forbids not only all the doctrines of the false religions but everything pertaining to them or in any way connected with them.

Again: "After the doings of the land of Egypt, wherein ye dwelt, shall ye not do: and after the doings of the land of Canaan...shall ye not do: neither shall ye walk in their ordinances." (Lev. 18:3) Both Egypt and Canaan had sunk to the lowest depths of moral and spiritual degradation. But their form of worship was attractive and imposing, and God's people were in constant danger of incorporating some of the pagan rites and ceremonies into their form of worship. The divine counsel was: Have nothing to do with the heathen customs and usages. "The doings" of

Two Systems of Worship

Egypt and Canaan, as such, would lead away from the worship of the true God.

Here is further admonition: "When the Lord thy God shall cut off the nations from before thee... and thou succeedest them, and dwellest in their land; take heed to thyself that thou be not snared by following them,...and that thou inquire not after their gods, saying, how did these nations serve their gods? Even so will I do likewise. Thou shalt not do so unto the Lord thy God." (Deut. 12:29-31)

When we study these divine injunctions, we can see how the God of heaven forbids not only the worship of false gods but the slightest deviation from the form of worship which, in His Word, He instituted and commanded. In no way can the Babylonian rites or ceremonies be assimilated. The true Christian church will be entirely separate from anything that issues from the alluring cup of Babylon. The pure fountain of truth from the Holy Bible will be adhered to by those who are followers of Christ. They will admit nothing into their doctrines or worship that does not bear the test of the "law and the testimony." For "all scripture is given by inspiration of God, and is profitable for doctrine, for reproof, for correction, for instruction in righteousness: that the man of God may be perfect, throughly furnished unto all good works." (2 Tim. 3:16, 17) These texts reveal the purpose of the Bible. It is for "doctrine." This means that if a church has doctrines that are not in harmony with what the Bible teaches, then that Church should lay aside the false beliefs and accept the doctrines of the Bible. When this is done, it is evidence that the "reproof," "correction," and "instruction" have been accepted. It is the duty of every church to search the Word of God to determine the veracity of their beliefs, and to be assured that all doctrines of theology which they hold are authoritatively based upon the Scripture.

The Wine of Roman Babylon

Does it really matter what we believe and how we worship? Here are the words of Christ:

"But in vain they do worship me, teaching for doctrines the commandments of men." Matt. 15:9 There is no saving power in man-made creeds. Why is man more susceptible to error than to truth? Why should a man be more eager to embrace dogmas which were conceived in ecumenical councils rather than what has been given by the inspiration of God? Strange infatuation indeed! God says: "I give you good doctrine, forsake ye not My law." (Prov.4:2)

Appendix to Chapter II

The Dutch Catechism

A NEW CATECHISM

Are the traditional dogmas of the Catholic Church going through a change? Some say Yes! while the vast majority would answer unequivocally NO! The Modern Roman Catholic may take refuge in the new *Dutch Catechism*, with its liberal views regarding the traditional beliefs of the church.

The *Dutch Catechism* is indeed a new volume in many respects. It was prepared by 150 Catholic theologians and sanctioned by the Dutch hierarchy. Its literary setting is more for the adult mind than for the immature mind of a child or a teen-ager. It is not written in the conventional way of questions and answers, but in essay form. There is definitely a departure from the dogmatic claims which are made by the long established catechisms, such as Butler's *Holy Family Catechism*; Deharbe, *A Complete Catechism of Catholic Religion*; Keenan, *A Doctrinal Catechism*; MacEachen, *Complete Catechism of Christian Doctrine; Baltimore Catechism*, which some catechists would like to update.

Has the new Dutch Catechism been accepted without any protest from the Vatican? A special papal commission was formed, with representatives of the Dutch hierarchy, on the possibility of having the book revised. As of this date I am not aware that any change in the original has been made. However, some members of the Roman Curia claimed to have found "in some 200 pages, 13 serious affirmations contrary to the faith and 48 minor errors."

I do not have a list of these "errors" and contradictions as charged by the Curia representatives. However, after examining this new volume, it is evident that it categorically and unequivocally contradicts the Holy Scriptures on the creation of Adam and Eve, our first parents. The uncertain notes that are sounded throughout the book give credence to the theory of evolution. Note the following regarding creation: "The account of creation, for instance, with its six days, is in poetic form. What it wishes to convey is that all things come from the hand of God. The form used is that of noble poetic imagery, not that of reporting. As early as the thirteenth century, St. Aquinas, for instance, pointed this out."[139] The six days of creation, which the Holy Bible records, must not be taken literally, according to the New Catechism. The events that took place those six days were nothing but "poetic imagery." Thus the Creator and His creative power are questioned, and the inspired record in the book of Genesis impugned. The teaching of evolution is designed to discredit the Bible.

But this new volume is not the first catechism to repudiate the account given of the six literal days of creation, each being a twenty-four-hour period. The sun is the ruling factor as to the length of a day. When the sun sets, the day ends and a new day begins. See Lev. 23:32 and Mark 1:32. Here is what a noted catechism states: "She [the church] has never, for instance, taught that the six days of creation mean days of twenty-four hours each."[140] If the church does not accept the record of creation given in the Bible, first and second chapters of Genesis, then there is nothing left but to believe in the hypothesis of evolution.

---

139   *A New Catechism*, Herder and Herder, Inc., 49.
140   Deharbe, 4.

The Dutch Catechism

This *New Catechism – Catholic Faith for Adults* does not include many of the precise dogmas which are found in the above list of catechisms. However, it cannot be said that the New Catechism, when dealing with Catholic traditional teachings, actually denies them. In a very artful way they are ignored. You look for enlightenment on a particular doctrine, and it is not even mentioned. Some dogmatic teachings which are found in authenticated Catholic published works and which have been taught, believed, and with severity have been enforced, are now regarded as a matter of <u>conscience</u>. Note the following:

> "There are many reasons why at the present time greater stress is laid on the personal verdict of conscience. There is a growing sense of the uniqueness of each man and of his situation. And we are living in a special period of transition when our sense of values is being very definitely renovated.
>
> "The question is all the more urgent where an antiquated sense of values is also an overnarrow one, or when laws which reflect an antiquated notion have gone too deeply into details. In such cases it is our duty to take counsel with our own instinct of faith, our own sense of what is good. (This of course will not be a solitary process. In the community of God, indeed, in the whole of mankind, one asks for advice, one discusses matters with others and one notes how a new notion takes form in consciences.)"[141]

What is the standard by which to test "our own instinct of faith?" Is the "conscience" a safe criterion when it comes to form a correct judgment respecting the Christian standards? How can a mind that is warped by wrong teachings, and a conscience that is seared by sin, determine what is truth and what is error? Without the divine rule it is impossible for sinful man to have a proper concept of right and wrong. This is the reason that the Ten Commandments were given by God, so that man would have a divine standard by which to measure truth and thus avoid the

---
[141] *A New Catechism*, 375.

pitfall of error. But does the New Catechism teach its students to accept unequivocally the Ten Commandments as the divine authoritative standard? Under the caption "Conscience Against the Commandments," note the following:

> "The discussion has helped us to see the primordial and profound unity of conscience and commandments. But there is another element to consider. They can and must come into conflict with one another. The law, the precise precept, cannot foresee exactly all circumstances. Cases will arise where one must do more or less than the law prescribes. Conscience, with its instinct for what is good here and now cannot simply let itself be guided by the letter of the law. it must sometimes even depart from the law in order to affirm in certain cases the ultimate moral values.
>
> "Another reason for a laudable tension is the development of our sense of values. There is a constant growth, as we saw, in our appreciation of good and evil. What at one time was the best possible expression of the great values of life (that is, of the ten commandments, which are radically unalterable) is seen later to be unsatisfactory. Conscience tries to reform and restate the law."[142]

Conscience and the Ten Commandments—do they "come into conflict with one another? Yes, if a person violates any one of the commandments, he certainly comes into conflict with the moral law. He is sinning against God; and if his violation involves any of the last six, he is also sinning against his neighbor. That faculty which distinguishes between right and wrong is used by the Holy Spirit to trouble the mind that an unlawful deed has been committed. It calls for repentance and not for the rejection of the law. How insidious is the teaching that a person's conscience "cannot simply let itself be guided by the letter of the law." How must our blessed Lord feel about such instruction given under the guise of Christianity?

---

[142] Ibid., 374.

The catechism also states that a person "must sometimes even depart from the law in order to affirm in certain cases the ultimate moral values." Where in the sacred Scriptures does the Lord give the license to break His immutable law? What could the circumstance be that would call for the ten holy precepts to be transgressed with impunity? What has happened to an individual who at one time had a regard for "the great values of life...the ten commandments," but finds them "later to be unsatisfactory"? The catechism states that his "conscience tries to reform and restate the law." It is his conscience that is in need of reform and not God's moral law.

The doctrine which this *New Catechism* advocates must be tested by the divine standard, which states: "To the law and to the testimony: if they speak not according to this word, it is because there is no light in them." (Isa. 8:20) There is "no light" in a church whose instruction will lead away from the Ten Commandments. We should, as Christians and lovers of our blessed Lord, be able to say: "Give me understanding, and I shall keep thy law; yea, I shall observe it with my whole heart. Make me to go in the path of thy commandments; for therein do I delight...So shall I keep thy law continually for ever and ever." (Ps. 119:34, 35, 44)

The Ten Commandments were written by our Lord on tables of stone: "And the Lord spake unto you out of the midst of the fire: ye heard the voice of the words...And He declared unto you His covenant, which He commanded you to perform, even ten commandments; and He wrote them upon two tables of stone." (Deut. 4:12, 13)

Counsel was given by our Lord to the people not to "add" nor "diminish" anything from the law, but they were to "keep" it. When any church or clergy teaches that God's law can be tampered with, it is quite evident that such is opposed to God and His Word: "Ye shall not add unto the word which I command you, neither shall ye diminish ought from it, that ye may keep the commandments of the Lord your God which I command you." (Deut. 4:2)

There is no place nor circumstance in the life of the true follower of Christ when conscience will "depart from the law." He will heed, under all provacation the instruction of Holy Writ: "Let us hear the conclusion of the whole matter: Fear God, and keep His commandments; for this is the whole duty of man." (Eccl. 13:13)

Appendix to Chapter III

Infant Baptism

Has the Catholic Church changed in respect to infant baptism? Here is what the *New Catechism* (Dutch) has to say on the subject:

"The child is christened at baptism. He is given the name of a saint, under whose particular protection he is placed...

"The baptism of a child is a sign of God's impatience. He is impatient to show that <u>every</u> new-born child is under God's call.

"Every child is for God. But then what happens to children who die without baptism?...The unbaptized adult can be saved if he fulfills faithfully his task in life and so shares although unconsciously in Christ's service. But unbaptized children are incapable even of this 'baptism of life.' What happens to them?"[143]

Before answering the question as to what happens to unbaptized children, the bishops of the Netherlands have this to say regarding the doctrine of infant baptism:

"There was great uncertainty in the church for a long time as regards the fate of unbaptized infants, because theologians considered the necessity of the baptism of water too <u>exclusively</u> from the point of view of its individual importance. Augustine, in a letter to Jerome, shows how keenly he felt the problem: 'When the question of the punishment of children is raised, it troubles me sorely, I assure you, and I am at a loss what to answer'.

"This was about A.D. 400. The great and humane Anselm was still uncertain about 1100. He cannot see how the infants

---

[143] Ibid., 251.

can be saved, but he goes on to say: 'I have spoken to the best of my capacity, making suggestions rather than affirmations, in the hope that at some time in the future God may teach me something better. But if anyone has a different opinion to put forward, I shall accept any view for which good reasons can be adduced.'

"In the course of the centuries, the Church has drawn on the ancient treasures of the faith to elaborate such reasons. It has become more and more clearly convinced that three truths must be borne in mind if the question is to be properly solved. The first is that God wills that all men should attain eternal blessedness. This certainly includes children, who are seen in the gospels as the special objects of God's love. The second truth is that Christ was born and died <u>for all</u>. And finally, we know that no one is lost except for sins which he has personally committed. In view of these truths, there must be a way by which unbaptized infants are saved," but they add, "We do not know exactly how."

The fact that the Bible does not sanction infant baptism, and the early fathers of the church as late as 1100 A.D. were in doubt regarding it, should have led the authors of the *New Catechism* to unequivocally expurgate it as a doctrine to be followed.

The Catholic Church is aware that a preparation of heart must precede the ordinance of baptism. How can a newborn infant be instructed? Sponsors are appointed to be responsible to see that the infant is instructed in the doctrine of the church. The Council of Trent limited the sponsors to "one godfather and one godmother." The *New Catechism* states the following:

"But the question is how can the child receive the sign of conversion and faith while it is still incapable of conversion and of the dedication of faith, for lack of mental equipment?

"The answer is that it receives the sign in the way it lives—in dependence on adults....Hence the baby is not baptized because it believes, but because we naturally wish

Infant Baptism

to pass on our faith. We bring the children within the circle of our own faith, into the faith of the Church."[144]

Can any human sponsor, be he ever so godly, "pass on" his "faith" to one who is incapable of believing or may not desire to be a Christian? Christ said: "Go ye into all the world, and preach the gospel to every creature. He that believeth and is baptized shall be saved; but he that believeth not shall be damned." (Mark 16:15,16)

When it comes to being saved, it is an individual matter. This is clearly revealed in the Scriptures. "Though Noah, Daniel, and Job, were in it, as I live, saith the Lord God, they shall deliver neither son nor daughter; they shall but deliver their own souls by their righteousness." (Ezek. 14:20)

False teaching is the result of not knowing what the Bible teaches. Christ, when confronted with a false doctrine from the religious teachers of His day, pointed out where the difficulty lay: "Jesus answered and said unto them, Ye do err, not knowing the scriptures, nor the power of God." (Matt. 22:29) If all would adhere strictly to the Holy Bible, there would be no false doctrines to mislead and no confusion relative to our salvation. Let us heed the admonition of Christ to "Search the scriptures, for...they are they which testify of Me." (John 5:39) What is needed most in the religious world is an intelligent understanding of the Sacred Scriptures.

---

[144] Ibid., 250.

The Wine of Roman Babylon

Appendix to Chapter IV

Auricular Confession

Has the New Catechism changed the doctrine of the auricular confession? In what way does it differ from the Catechism of the Council of Trent?

The approach may be different, but the doctrine is the same. It is true that the bishops of the Netherlands elaborated on the nature of sin and the division between "mortal" and "venial" sins. But they have given support to the church in its right to forgive sins.

Note the following: "His own authority to forgive was given to the Church by our Lord as an Easter gift...The Church is the place where God's pardon is given to men. The Church has been given full authority to forgive."[145]

How does the church forgive sin? "We confess our sins to a priest...Our Lord has in fact entrusted his power of forgiving sins to the hierarchical Church...The confession of sins is not in conflict with the situation of the sinner. It is, on the contrary, very fitting...The Confessor is not there just to listen passively. He has also, in a certain sense, a judicial function."[146]

This "judicial function" is carried out by the priest in the confessional as the penitent confesses his guilt. This is known as "sacramental confession," which results in "sacramental absolution."

---

[145] Ibid., 454, 456.
[146] Ibid., 460, 461.

While the Catechism mentions the trend of confessing "one's guilt in a common liturgical assembly," yet it makes clear that such a confession is not sacramental. Therefore, the doctrine of the auricular (or ear) confession has not been changed.

Appendix to Chapter V

Penance

Have the authors of the *New Catechism* changed the Sacrament of Penance? Have they digressed in any way from the traditional teachings of the Church which issued a comprehensive manual for Parish Priests following the Council of Trent? Here are a few statements taken from that volume:

> "The sinner, then, who repents, casts himself humbly and sorrowfully at the feet of the priest...In the priest, who is his legitimate judge, he venerates the person and the power of Christ our Lord; for in the administration of the Sacrament of Penance, as in that of the other Sacraments, the priest holds the place of Christ...For there is no sin, however great or horrible, which cannot be effaced by the Sacrament of Penance, and that not merely once, but over and over again."[147]

Let us now go to the *New Catechism* to find if the Sacrament of Penance is still to be imposed by the priest upon the penitent:

> "After hearing the penitent's sins, the confessor imposes a penance. In the conviction of Jesus' overwhelming grace, the penance is usually disproportionately small. Jesus has made good our sins, not we ourselves...Still, the penance should not be so small as to be comic. Three Hail Marys seems hardly fitting. If a pentitent has confessed to speaking ill of his neighbor, he should be told to say something to correct the impression. If he has been secretly unfaithful to his marriage vows, he should be told to find some way of being

---

[147] *Catechism of the Council of Trent*, 269, 270.

specially good to his wife. A possible penance would be the reading of a part of Scripture relevant to the confession (the Sermon on the Mount, for instance).[148]

It is quite evident that the Dutch bishops have not changed this fourth Sacrament. Penance must be imposed on the penitent by the confessor.

However, there is one aspect of innovation that deserves a comment, and that is where, under certain circumstances, penance imposed includes Scripture reading. Should the reading of Holy Scripture be regarded as penance, as an act of self-abasement performed to indicate a sorrow for sin? No! It should be a delight to read and study the Word of God. We should approach the Bible with the same attitude that Jeremiah had when he wrote: "Thy words were found, and I aid eat them; and thy word was unto me the joy and rejoicing of mine heart." (Jer. 15:16)

The bishops of the Netherlands advocated for the penitent, as part of his penance, the reading of the Sermon on the Mount. This portion of Holy Scripture should not only be read but studied, and its divine principles strictly obeyed. The Catechism states: "If a penitent has confessed to speaking ill of his neighbor, he should be told to say something to correct the impression." If the penitent were to read what our Lord advocated in the Sermon on the Mount, with respect to dealing with his injured neighbor, his approach would be different from what the Catechism states. Jesus said, "If thou bring thy gift to the altar, and there rememberest that thy brother hath aught against thee; leave there thy gift before the altar, and go thy way; first be reconciled to thy brother, and then come and offer thy gift." (Matt. 5:23, 24) Then instead of going to the priest to confess, we are to go to the one whom we have injured and acknowledge our sin, and ask his forgiveness. if we

---

[148] *New Catechism*, 461, 462.

have in any manner defrauded him, restitution should be made. When the divine command of Christ is faithfully carried out, then true repentance and not penance is manifest.

The Wine of Roman Babylon

Appendix to Chapter VI

The Mass

Since the Second Vatican Council, various clergy and laymen have given thought to the Eucharistic Sacrifice, and how and where it can be celebrated. Consideration has been given to litergical change and also to the active participation of the laity.

In recent years the Church has shown an increasing tendency to relax some of her discipline regarding the Eucharistic Fast. The traditional period of the fast was from the previous midnight, and its observance was virtually universal. Pope Pius XII in his Apostolic Constitution, "Christus Dominus", January 16, 1953, and his "Sacram Communionem" of March 19, 1957, changed the total abstinence to the granting permission to drink water at any time. A three-hour fast from solid food and alcoholic drink and a one-hour fast from non-alcoholic liquid was to be observed by those who were to receive Holy Communion. Pope Paul VI, on November 21, 1964, further reduced the period of fasting before the reception of the Sacraments to one hour instead of the three-hour imposed by Pius XII. So the Eucharistic Fast has been changed by two Popes.

For centuries the Mass was celebrated only in the forenoon. It can now be celebrated in the P.M. (post meridiem) for the convenience of those who otherwise could not attend church in the forenoon.

The liturgical changes that were initiated by Pope Pius XII have developed a new code of rules for the Church. Growth is evident in the liturgical movement since the

The Wine of Roman Babylon

Second Vatican Council. Changes were made in the feast days, some being eliminated, while others were transferred to other dates. Examine the Old Calendar of the Saints, and we would agree that it needed to have some of the feast days eliminated.

But why not do away with all of them? The New Testament has nothing to say about feast days of obligation, or of days set apart in which any human should be honored, revered, or implored. The Holy Scriptures state: "Put not your trust in princes, nor in the son of man, in whom there is no help. His breath goeth forth, he returneth to his earth; in that very day his thoughts perish." Psalm 146:3,4 In fact, a "curse" is pronounced upon the man whose trust for salvation is in the human: "Thus saith the Lord; Cursed be the man that trusteth in man, and maketh flesh his arm...Blessed is the man that trusteth in the Lord, and whose hope the Lord is."(Jer.17: 5, 7)

Appendix to Chapter VII

Omission of the Cup

The *New Catechism* has much to say regarding Holy Communion and how it should be celebrated. However, the ancient custom of receiving Holy Communion under the two species of bread and wine has not been mentioned. Emphasis is given to the celebration of the Eucharistic under one specie—the bread. The Catechism is silent on the existing practice of the Church in restricting the wine from the laity, and permitting only the celebrating priest to partake.

The subject of Communion in both kinds was evident during the Second Vatican Council. A desire to restore the Chalice to the laity was considered, particularly on occasions such as marriage. *The Congregation of Rites*, March 7, 1965, listed the occasions in which bishops could permit reception in both kinds; it even stipulated four alternatives of drinking from the chalice, using a spoon, or a tube, or by intinction—dipping the bread in the chalice.

How many bishops are bringing their dioceses into harmony with the Biblical teaching on the administration of the sacraments in both species is not known. It is quite obvious that adherence is given to the Council of Trent rather the the Second Vatican Council.

The Wine of Roman Babylon

Appendix to Chapter VIII

Masses and Purgatory

What has the *New Catechism* to say on the subject of Purgatory?

First, I wish to state that the official teaching of the Church on the doctrince of Purgatory was defined at the Council of Lyons (1274). There arose certain questions from the Greeks regarding the conceptive idea of material fire and the difference between guilt and penalty inflicted on an offender as a divine retribution.

The Reformation was in opposition to the doctrine of purgatory as it made of none effect the plan of redemption by our Saviour. Such teaching was in direct contradiction of the Holy Scriptures, the students of the Bible declared.

The Council of Trent (1545–1563) reaffirmed the doctrine of Purgatory set forth by the Councils of Lyons and Florence. But it must be remembered that the nature of duration of the purgatorial purification has never received domatic definition by any Council. The church encourages the offerings of Masses for the dead, private prayers, and works of devotion on behalf of the souls in Purgatory.

Has any modification taken place that would point to the vicarious, atoning death of Christ, once for all, for the redemption of mankind? What comfort and hope is given to the conscientious Catholic who is facing death? His venial sins must be expurgated either by good works on earth or in the fires of Purgatory after death. Is the Memento in the canon of the Mass for the dead still being carried out? If so, no change has been made. But let us examine the *New Catechism* as to what it has to say on this subject.

Under the title "Repairing the Damage" is the following:

"Firstly, because the thought of making reparation accompanies repentance and forgiveness. This can sometimes take a very practical form, as in restitution after theft. Where this is impossible ... the penitent will try to make up for it in some way or other, by some good act. The offender also feels the desire to suffer for what he has done—to do penance. These things have been described in various ways in the tradition of the forgiveness of sins in the Church: reparation, restitution, good works, penitential works, the temporal punishment for sin to be expiated in purgatory. In former times, the penance imposed could be replaced by useful good works. Instead of going on pilgramage to Jerusalem, the penitent built a bridge for travellers...Such customs were at the origin of indulgences. A good work could replace penance, and later, 'the temporal punishment due to sin,' and the difference was made up from the treasury of the merits of the saints,' which the Church besought God to draw on. The element of faith of permanent value behind these antiquated customs is that the Church tries to bestow largesse as royally as possible from the treasure of Christ's forgiveness, and that we do something which embodies our good will."[149]

From the above it is clear that the authors of the Dutch Catechism believe in reparation and meritorious works in this life to atone for our sins, and the final expiation in Purgatory. Note what is said relative to the "Purification of the Dead":

"Prayer for the dead is a tradition of the Church. Why is it offered? It is offered because there is still so much bad will, indifference and rebellion in man, even when he dies in grace. (Would any of us feel that he is ready to enter heaven just as he is?) There is still much ingrained egoism to be

---
149   Ibid., 455.

Masses and Purgatory

converted, cleansed away and purified. This takes place in death. To die is also to die to evil. it is the baptism of death along with Christ, in which the baptism of water is completed. The other face of this death—as the Church believes—can be a purification, the definitive, total conversion to God's light. How long does this process last? We must remember once more that all this takes place outside time as we know it ... But from our point of view there is a certain time during which we regard someone as 'departed.'

We help him by our prayers. How many months or years it is we cannot tell. It depends on a man's life."[150]

If God requires the temporal punishment for sin in the fires of Purgatory, most certainly the Bible would have something to say. But it is strangely silent. The Catholic Church must go to an uninspired source to support their Masses, prayers, and meritorious work for the dead. The Catechism speaks of the Memento in these words:

"In the canon of the Mass every day there is a place provided where the names of the faithful departed may be mentioned, in the middle of the community's act of worship, in the middle of the celebration of the sacrifice of the cross. After the mention of those who are prayed for, the following prayer is said: 'To these O Lord, and to all who repose in Christ, grant, we beseech you, a place of refreshment, light and peace.' 2 November is a day of special intercession of the dead."[151]

November 2, All Souls' Day, is still being observed in the Church. Prayer for the dead goes back to St. Odilio of Cluny in 998. He fixed the date of All Souls' on November 2. Masses are still being offered for the repose of the souls departed. The revenue that results from this feast is indeed great and too lucrative to be abolished.

But what does all this do to our Lord and Saviour and His atoning sacrifice? When the efficacy of His blood is applied, the sins are removed, both <u>mortal</u> and <u>venial</u>. May we heed

---

[150] Ibid., 476, 477.
[151] Ibid., 477.

the voice of God saying to each of us: "Come now, and let us reason together, saith the Lord: though your sins be as scarlet, they shall be as white as snow; though they be red like crimson, they shall be as wool." (Isa.1:18) "If we confess our sins, he is faithful and just to forgive us our sins, and to cleanse us from all unrighteousness." (1 John 1:9)

The venial sins He will pardon as well as the mortal. Yes, and He does it without money or meritorious works, so the rich have no advantage over the poor: "Ho, every one that thirsteth, come ye to the waters, and he that hath no money; come...Incline your ear, and come unto me, hear, and your soul shall live." (Isaiah 55:1, 3) There is no mention in Holy Scripture of expiatory suffering after death to atone for any of our sins, be they mortal or venial. Thank God, Christ has paid the full price!

Appendix to Chapter IX

Peter and the Rock

The *New Catechism* has not given much space to the Apostle Peter. What is written would not fill one page. One would think that a man elevated to such a high rank in the church would have been given more space. But the Catechism leaves no doubt but that the Apostle Peter is the rock upon which the church is built:

> "Then come, the words, which in Matthew 18 are also addressed to the Apostles in general, 'to bind' and 'to loose,' that is, to declare right and wrong, also to excommunicate or to lift the ban—with effect 'in heaven', that is, 'with God.' This power is here bestowed on Peter alone, the weak, impulsive and very ordinary Peter, the rock which still has to be hewn and chiselled by Jesus with many a hard word."[152]

If so much power were entrusted to the Apostle Peter, why was it not mentioned in the sacred writings? Nothing is found in the works of Luke regarding any regency being conferred upon Peter. Luke, who wrote the book of Acts, gives the account of selecting a man to fill the vacancy left by Judas: "And they gave forth their lots; and the lot fell upon Matthias; and he was numbered with the eleven apostles."(Acts 1:26) If Peter held the supremacy, he did not exercise it on this occasion. Matthias was chosen by the eleven and was coequal with the eleven apostles.

Again we find in the selecting of the first seven deacons that Peter did not exercise any superiority in this matter.

---
[152] Ibid., 143.

The Wine of Roman Babylon

(Acts 6:1-6) When the first church council was held to deal with important issues that had arisen, it was not Peter who was the convocator, nor was he the one who occupied the chair at this council. James had the final word. Peter, if pope, did not wield his sovereign prerogative. (Acts 15: 13, 19, 20)

The Apostle Paul, who wrote fourteen books of the New Testament, makes no reference to a pontificate. Most surely he would have known if the primacy were conferred on Peter. Paul disclaims inferiority in these words: "For I suppose I was not a whit behind the very chiefest apostles." (2 Cor. 11:5) He did not say the chief apostle, but "apostles," thus recognizing the equality of all. We have on record Paul reproving Peter before the church. (see Gal. 2:11-14) Paul would never have been guilty of such a flargrant act against Peter were he occupying the apostolic see. Paul addressed a long letter to the Roman Christians and mentioned many names but neglected to name the Roman pontiff. If a pontifical office had been established by Christ, with the Apostle Peter occupying it, Paul knew nothing of it.

We have two ecclesiastical publications from the pen of Peter, but neither one mentions his vice-regal authority. The books by James, Jude, and John are silent on the primacy of St. Peter. The apostle loved his Lord and suffered martyrdom, as did all of the apostles with the exception of John. If is one thing to claim Apostolic Succession. It is another thing to live as did the apostles.

No, Christ never built His church upon Peter, or any of the apostles. The true church is built upon the immovable Rock—Christ Jesus—and "the gates of hell shall not prevail against it."

Appendix to Chapter X

Peter and the Keys

Has the church changed its attitude toward the primacy of St. Peter and the apostolic succession? Has the superiority of rank long conceded and claimed by the bishops of Rome been challenged by the ecclesiarch of Holland when they produced the *New Catechism*? Did the men who wrote this volume work on the principle that the office of a bishop depended alone on the political rank and social position of the city in which he lived?

Because a bishop was appointed to the ancient city of Rome, with its political importance, did this give him the divine right of supremacy in consequence of his claiming to be the successor of St. Peter? To support this claim the church has asserted, without a shadow of scriptural or historical proof, that Peter was the first bishop of Rome, and was constituted by Jesus Christ as supreme head of the church upon earth. For the Catholic Church this is a very fundamental doctrine, and any digression from its validity would be counted heretical by it.

It is not surprising to find that the New Catechism has little to say on the subject of Peter being the exclusive possessor of "the keys of the kingdom of heaven." But the matter is not ignored. Note this terse statement:

> "Heaven, too, has its gates, and their invisible keys are in Peter's hands. He is the steward with full authority, with the function of regent as described in Isaiah 22: 21-22."[153]

---
[153] Ibid., 143.

These words are without obscurity or ambiguity. Peter has "full authority, with its function of regent," and is invested with vicarious jurisdiction to heaven. What a position!

Under the heading "Unity Through the Successor of Peter," the Catechism has this to say regarding the pope:

"The special task of the bishop of Rome is that of Peter; to be the principle of unity in the Church, to keep it one in faith and life. For this purpose, the bishop of Rome is the authoritative head of the college of bishops. He is not placed above the bishops, but as the first among them and the one who gives directives. In this sense, he is of course above them, just as a head belongs to the body and still is above it. He has been called Pope (i.e. Father, from the late Greek papas), since the fourth century. As ruler and teacher, he is the head of the Church."[154]

The supposed infallibility of the pope is given a brief space in the *New Catechism*. The Dutch authors were careful how they set forth pontifical infallibility:

"The unifying function of the Pope entails an important task as teacher. As head of the college of bishops, he possesses infallibility in a special measure. He is the beacon. This does not mean that he can proclaim dogmas apart from the Church. He can only declare what the Church universal believes. He takes counsel with all the Catholic bishops, particularly with the Synod of Bishops instituted since the Second Vatican Counsel. But since union with the Pope is the touchstone for belonging to the unity, an utterance of the Pope is certainly full of the truth of God's Spirit, at least when he affirms explicitly (which happens rarely) that he is speaking infallibly and binding all Christians. This charism (freely-given grace of the spirit for the general good) is linked with the office of being first among his brothers. — As regards the faith of the Pope, he is a believer who receives his faith, even as Pope, from the fellowship of the Church in which he has such an important task to perform."[155]

---
154 Ibid., 367.
155 Ibid., 368.

If the pope is "head of the infallible college of bishops," and he "possesses infallibility," why is he not qualified to "proclaim dogmas apart from the Church?" If "he can only declare what the church universal believes," what advantage is there to infallibility? To claim ecclesiastical inerrability when dealing with faith and morals is an absurdity. There is only One who is perfect

Jesus Christ — and He has given us a perfect guide — the Holy Scriptures — to go by. They never err when speaking on faith and morals. They also are an infallible guide to doctrine.

The intellectual weakness of man shows clearly the absurdity of the claim of infallibility. Human reason, weak in its operations and blinded by passion, prepossessions, and selfishness, is open to the inroads of error. Facts testify its fallibility. Liability to error, with respect to each individual regardless of his position in life, is universally admitted. The Catholic Church, like other churches, is made up of clergy and laity. Such are subject to human weakness and mistakes, individually and collectively. How can fallible individuals therefore, though united, ever form an infallible church?

"With the instruction given in the Bible, all may have an enerrant guide, unsullied by human pride, passion, or prejudice: "All scripture is given by inspiration of God, and is profitable for doctrine, for reproof, for correction, for instruction in righteousness: That the man of God may be perfect, throughly furnished unto all good works." (2 Tim. 3:16, 17)

The Wine of Roman Babylon

Appendix to Chapter XI

The Immaculate Conception

According to the Dutch bishops, the question of Mary's immaculate conception is an established fact. Without either Biblical or historical evidence, they assert that the virgin Mary was immaculately conceived. However, they acknowledge that it took the church a long time to arrive at this conclusion:

> "This happy conviction of the superiority of grace is brought out very forcibly in a truth which only became clear to the Church in a long, slow process. Thomas Aquinas and Bernard still could not see how it could be properly asserted. But the Church arrived gradually at this truth by meditating on the whole of revelation and solemnly defined it in the last century. It is the truth that Mary was free from the guilt of original sin. She was conceived immaculate. Living in a sinful world, she shared the pain of the world, but not its wickedness. She is our sister in suffering, but not in evil. She overcame evil completely by good. This was of course entirely due to Christ's redemption."[156]

This belated doctrine of the church was not "defined" until 1854. How did the people serve God without the knowledge of Mary's immaculate state all those intervening years?

Again we read: "Mary has a special place."

This is not stated, to begin with, as 'doctrine', but simply as a fact which may be observed. In the Christianity of the East and of the West she is present more than any other

---
[156] Ibid., 268.

person, except of course Christ. Her presence is to be felt even in our houses, not just through the icons with the expressive eyes or the pictures with the gentle smile, but above all because she is spoken to and because prayers to her are heard by God... It is more important that the Church as a whole has recognized her glory so much as a part of its faith that it has expressly proclaimed that Mary has already been raised from the dead, body and soul. Of the other dead we may only say that they will be made alive, they are about to arise, but we acknowledge that Mary is already glorified. it is true that her glory—like that of Christ himself—will only be perfect when the whole of mankind is gathered together.

> "Just as Christ's resurrection is effective among us through his forceful, vivid presence in the life of the world, so too, we may say, the glory or the 'Assumption' of Mary. This means that she is more in the world than any other woman. Cleopatra is remembered. Mary is addressed. She is the most closely present of all women. The risen Christ and Mary assumed into heaven—the true Adam and the true Eve of mankind—are not to be sought far away from us, as though heaven were an immense theatre full of purely spiritual souls where only two places were bodily occupied, those of Christ and Mary...We can experience the presence of Christ and Mary by living on earth in the Spirit of Christ and by speaking to them in prayer."[157]

The above statements show clearly where the *New Catechism* stands on the subject of Mary. Not only has the doctrine of the "Immaculate Conception" been discussed and endorsed, but her assumption has been confirmed, and all without one word from the Holy Scriptures. No, the virgin Mary is not in heaven. She is in the grave, waiting for the resurrection—when there will be no sickness, sorrow, or anything that would lead us away from the true God. The first commandment is being violated: "Thou shalt have no other gods before Me." (Exod. 20:3) Again, "I

---
[157] Ibid., 475, 476.

The Immaculate Conception

am the Lord: that is my name: and my glory will I not give to another, neither my praise to graven images." (Isa. 42:80 May we accept what the Holy Scriptures say and give glory to God and not to a human.

The Wine of Roman Babylon

Appendix to Chapter XII

Invocation of Saints

What are the changes that have come into the church since Vatican Council II? Changes have taken place in the liturgy but not in the dogmas of the church. Feasts of saints have been affected somewhat, due to the elimination of some saints from the calendar. Pope Paul is responsible for some of these changes, due to various reasons. Note the following:

"Commenting on the elimination of some feasts, *L'Osservatore Della Domenica*, the Vatican City weekly said: 'Generally, the removal of a name from the calendar does not mean passing judgment on the nonexistence (of a saint) or lack of holiness. Many (saints) have been removed (from the calendar) because all that remains certain about them is their name, and this would say too little to the faithful in comparison with many others.'"[158]

The reform carried out by Pope Paul may have disturbed the devotee who had his popular saint either of the following—St. Christopher, St. Nicholas, St. Valentine, St. George, and St. Barbara. In May of 1969 the Vatican announced the removal of them with other saints from the calendar. However, they remain in the official list of saints. The fact that some saints have been dropped while others have been added does not alter the attitude of the church toward the doctrine of the Invocation of Saints. Pope Paul canonized over fifty between 1964 and 1974.[159]

---
158 *1975 Catholic Almanac* (Huntington, Indiana: Our Sunday Visitor, Inc.), 285.
159 Ibid., 80.

The Wine of Roman Babylon

The *New Catechism* voices its sanction on this subject: "All who have died, belonging to the fellowship of the human race and to the fellowship of the Church, all the good from the apostles, martyrs and saints to the least of believers, now live in God. And therefore the Church recognizes that they are joined to us in some way."[160]

The litanies are still in force, and deceased saints are invoked to pray for the suppliant. "There are seven litanies approved for liturgical use: Litanies of Loreto (Litany of the Blessed Mother), the Holy Name, All Saints, the Sacred Heart, the Precious Blood, St.Joseph, Litany for the Dying."[161]

So the Virgin Mary, St. Joseph and All Saints are implored to "pray for us." All Saints' Day, November 1, is a holy day of obligation and is still recognized by the church. The Catechism has this to say:

> "The work of God's Spirit in the lives of men is celebrated in the liturgy by the feasts of the saints—their 'birthday feasts' which are here the day of their death. Personalities of the most various types are thus commemorated in the liturgy of the Church year. The feast of all those who allowed themselves to be led by the Holy Spirit is celebrated on a single day, 1 November—'All Saints.'"[162]

The church has not changed this doctrine. Her members still offer their invocatory prayer for help from the deceased ones. May we adhere to what God says in Holy Scripture: "Put not your trust in princes, nor in the son of man, in whom there is no help. His breath goeth forth, he returneth to the earth; in that very day his thoughts perish." (Ps. 146:3, 4)

---

160   *New Catechism*, 475.
161   *1975 Catholic Almanac*, 366.
162   *New Catechism*, 200.

Appendix to Chapter XIII

The Immortality of the Soul

The authors of the *New Catechism* are not very clear as to what actually happens at death. The indefiniteness of their teaching on this subject can be attested to by the following:

"And where are those we love now, immediately after their death?...Up to quite recent times, a solution was often sought in the simple distinction between 'body' and 'soul.' After death, it was thought, the soul continues to exist separately while the body perishes. At the last judgment, the body is gathered from the clay. This clear picture was an effort to render faithfully the data of the Bible. But an effort must be made to express them otherwise, for the following reasons. The new effort at expression is not a change of faith, but a somewhat different way of interpreting the same faith ... our Lord means that there is something of man, that which is most properly himself, which can be saved after death. This 'something' is not the body which is left behind. But our Lord does not say that this which is truly man is entirely disassociated from a new body. It is not biblical usage to speak of a purely disembodied soul of man."[163]

The writers admit that: "The new effort at expression is not a change in the faith, but a somewhat different way of interpreting the same faith." On the Immortality of the Soul the Catholic Dictionary states:

Here there is a marked divergence of opinion among Catholic philosophers. St. Thomas and many who follow him believe that it can be proved by reason, Scotus, on the

---
163   Ibid., 473.

contrary, regards it as a truth cognisable by faith alone... Origen held with Plato that souls existed before they were united with the body...Putting this aside, we find that at least three distinct theories on the origin of the soul have been held in the Church."[164]

We find in the *New Catechism* a blending of all three philosophies. Those who accept the doctrine of the natural immortality of the soul have lost sight of the atheistical, and unscriptural doctrine on which it rests. The authors, in handling this subject, reveal their confusion and their imperfect understanding of Holy Scripture. Note the following:

"All who have died, belonging to the fellowship of the Church, all the good from the apostles, martyrs and saints to the least of believers, now live in God. And therefore the Church recognizes that they are joined to us In some way. In this union of life in God and with us, Mary has a very special place."[165]

Such indistinct teaching is essentially mystical, and consequently unsupported by the Holy Scriptures: "Jesus answered and said unto them, Ye do err, not knowing the scriptures, nor the power of God." (Matt. 22:29) The Bible plainly states that "the dead know not anything." (Eccl. 9:5-6) They rest in the grave until the Second Coming of Christ. (See John 5:28, 29; 1 Thess. 4:16-17; 1 Cor. 15:51-53) The hope we have should be based upon the Word of God and not on the philosophy of treacherous errors, whether found in an old or New Catechism or in the archives of a church.

---

164 Wm. E. Addis and Thomas Arnold, 771.
165 *New Catechism*, 475.

Appendix to Chapter XIV

Eternal Torment in Hell

The *New Catechism*, when dealing with the subject of an eternal hell, deals with it in an exquisitely sensitive manner. In fact there is no doctrine in the entire volume that received the delicate touch and the avoidance of personal endorsement as that of eternal fire. Instead they call it "eternal sin." Here are a few excerpts:

"Jesus speaks of the possibility of one's being eternally condemned. We read of 'eternal punishment' (Matt. 25:46). This could he wrongly understood, as if a disaster or even an injustice than befell the damned, as can sometimes happen with punishments on earth. Hence we find it more enlightening to express the same truth by the term 'eternal sin.' The state of cold obstinacy has become eternal ...To be lost means to be entirely closed in on oneself, without contact with others or with God. This is the punishment, the 'second death.' (Rev. 20:14)...

"We sometimes think that hell is impossible to reconcile with the love of God...Each of us must draw his own conclusions here. The warning given by Christ is a blessing for us. Saints too have believed in hell, without finding it in contradiction with God's love.

"For those who harden themselves, the tender warmth of God's love becomes forever a fire of remorse and embittered resentment."[166]

Note the expressions: "Eternal punishment" could be "wrongly understood." Instead of eternal fire it is "eternal sin." "To be lost means to be entirely closed in on oneself."

---
166   Ibid., 480, 481.

The Wine of Roman Babylon

What does this mean? Their answer is: "The second death." But I must admit that I am still puzzled. Such ambiguous statements do not reflect the true gospel as given in the inspired Word of God. How is the word "hell" defined? "Hell: The state of punishment of the damned — i.e., those who die in mortal sin, in a condition of self-alienation from God and of opposition to the divine plan of salvation. The punishment of hell begins immediately after death and lasts forever."[167]

This volume is "published with Ecclesiastical Approval," and is an up-to-date statement of the Church.

The *New Catechism* is at variance with the teachings of the Church on the subject of hell. The nature of hell fire has never been defined by the Church. St. Augustine avows his ignorance regarding the nature of the fire of Hell. St. Thomas Aquinas described the fire not in terms of burning lost souls, but rather to confining and imprisoning. This is the position taken by the Dutch theologians, which accounts for the paradoxical statements made on this subject.

---

[167] *1975 Catholic Almanac*, 361.

Appendix to Chapter XV

Extreme Unction

Peter Lombard (1100-1160), an Italian theologian, bishop of Paris, was the first known author to use the term "extreme unction." The Constitution of Liturgy of the Second Vatican Council recommended the title "Annointing of the Sick." It was Pope Paul VI who authorized a revision of the rite. It was approved Nov. 30, 1973. The Pope ordered the new rite into effect as of Jan. 1, 1974. The new title is "Sacred Anointing of the Sick." The former name—"extreme unction"—has been dropped.

Other changes have taken place that are worthy of note in respect to the oil. Normally oil blessed by the bishop on Maundy Thursday is used in the anointing, but in case of necessity the priest administering the Sacrament may bless the oil. In the past only olive oil was required, but oil from a vegetable source may now be used if necessary.

The *New Catechism* fully endorses the sacrament:

"As soon as sickness takes a grave turn, the priest should be called to anoint the sick...Very often, on receiving this sacrament, the sick person actually experiences a revival of strength. As well as being a preparation for death, the sacrament may in fact be a preparation for life...

"The priest anoints the eyelids, ears, nose, mouth, lips, hands, and feet (or in case of necessity, merely the forehead)...

"The family should prepare a table, or a corner of a table, in the sickroom, covered with a white cloth on which there should be a crucifix and two lighted candles. They should also provide a little bowl of holy water and a sprinkler (such as a sprig of greenery), and another little bowl of ordinary water. The priest will bring the rest."[168]

What similarity is there between the way in which the sacrament Anointing of the Sick is conducted and that which is written in the epistle of James 5:14, 15? There is no mention of the oil being applied to the various parts of the body. Neither does it list the furnishings of the room in which the rite is to be conducted. Why make a simple service so complicated and mystical?

It is quite obvious that the *New Catechism* is in accord with the Constitution on Liturgy of the Second Vatical Council, and has approved the revised rites of the change of title "Anointing of the Sick," and the administration of the Eucharist to sick persons.

---

[168] *New Catechism*, 469, 470.

Appendix to Chapter XVI

Sunday Observance

The Catechism of the Council of Trent takes the position that the Sabbath commandment is the only one of the ten that is alterable. The other nine commandments are "obligatory at all times and unalterable," but not the fourth commandment, it was subject to change. It further declares: "But the Church of God has thought it well to transfer the celebration and observance of the Sabbath to Sunday."[169]

No Scripture proof for Sunday observance states a Catholic author, Rt. Rev. John Milner: "The first Precept in the Bible is that of sanctifying the seventh day: 'God blessed the *seventh day*, and sanctified it.' (Gen.2:3) This precept was confirmed by God in the ten commandments: 'Remember the Sabbath-day, to keep it holy. The *seventh day* is the Sabbath of the Lord thy God.' (Exod. 20) On the other hand, Christ declares that He is *not come to destroy the law, but to fulfill it.* (Matt.5:17) He Himself observed the Sabbath: 'and, as His custom was, He went into the synagogue on the Sabbath day.' (Luke 4:16) His disciples likewise observed it after His death: *'They rested on the Sabbath day according to the commandment,'* (Luke 23:56) Yet with all this weight of Scripture authority for keeping the Sabbath, or seventh day, holy, Protestants of all denominations make this a *profane day*, and transfer the obligation of it to the *first day of the week*, or the *Sunday*. Now what

---

[169] *Catechism of the Council of Trent*, 402.

The Wine of Roman Babylon

authority have they for doing this? None whatever, except the *unwritten word,* or *tradition,* of the Catholic Church."[170]

The following is from an historical source: "Sunday (Dies Solis, of the Roman Calendar: 'day of the sun,' because dedicated to the sun), the first day of the week, was adopted by the early Christians as a day of worship. The 'sun' of Latin adoration they interpreted as the 'Sun of Righteousness.'...No regulations for its observance are laid down in the New Testament, nor, indeed, is its observance even enjoined."[171]

The *New Catechism* has written in support of Sunday observance:

> "Not to have to work is an almost divine feeling. Sunday, the Lord's Day is meant in this way. It is to be a day of festival, of being something more than human...The Sabbath was made for man, not man for the sabbath.' (Mark 2:27) Since New Testament times Christians have chosen the day of the resurrection as the Lord's Day. The day after the sabbath was when they came together and celebrated Eucharist, and later, took their solemn weekly rest."[172]

The authors of the *New Catechism* were probably careful to avoid offending their "separate brethren" by not acknowledging the vital part that the Catholic Church had in changing the Sabbath to the first day of the week; in fact, they are strangely silent on the whole matter. *The Catholic Mirror* of Dec. 23, 1893, states unequivocally that Sunday is a Roman Catholic institution which is in opposition to the Bible. Note the following:

> "The only recourse left the Protestants is either to retire from Catholic territory, wherever they have been squatting for three and a half centuries, and accept their own teacher, the Bible, in good faith,...commence forthwith to keep the Saturday—the day enjoined by the Bible as their sole

---

170   John Milner, *End of Religious Controversy* (New York: P. J. Kenedy, 1897), 89.
171   *Schaff-Herzog Encyclopedia.*
172   *New Catechism,* 320.

teacher, cease to be squatters, and a living contradiction of their own principles, or, take out letters of adoption as citizens of the kingdom of Christ on earth, His church (Catholic), and be no longer victims of self-delusions and necessary self-contradiction!

"The arguments contained in this pamphlet are firmly grounded on the word on God, and, having closely studied wtih the Bible in hand, leave no escape for the conscientious Protestant except the abandonment of Sunday worship and return to Saturday, commanded by their teacher the Bible; or, unwilling to abandon the traditions of the Catholic Church, which enjoins the keeping of Sunday, and which they have accepted in direct opposition to their teacher, the Bible, consistently accept her in all her teaching. Reason and common sense demand the acceptance of one or the other of these alternatives; Either Protestantism or the keeping of Sunday."

Compromise is impossible.

The Catholic is not impressed when he sees the devotion of his Protestant neighbor to the observance of Sunday. It is an evidence to him that the Church and not the Bible is to be obeyed. Can any church or human change God's holy law? God's Word of Truth — the Bible — cannot be changed by man; it stands immortalized. "For ever, O Lord, thy word is settled in heaven." (Ps. 119:89) "My covenant will I not break, nor alter the thing that is gone out of my lips." (Ps.89:34) We are dealing with an unchangeable God: "For I am the Lord, I change not." (Mal.3:6) Christ is the one who said: "The Scripture cannot be broken." (John 10:35) In the last book of the Bible we have the warning not to add or take away from what God wrote: "If any man shall take away from the words of the book of this prophecy, God shall take away his part out of the book of life." (Rev. 22:19)

Bibliography

BOOKS

ADDIS, WM. E., and THOMAS ARNOLD. *A Catholic Dictionary.* 2nd edition. London: Kegan Paul, Trench & Company, 1884.

BELLARMINE, CARDINAL ROBERT. *Disputationes de Controversiis Christianae Fidei adversus Hujus Temporis Haereticos.* Venice: J. Malachinus, 1721.

BOULLAN, JOSEPH A. *The Life of the Blessed Virgin Mary.* New York City: P. J. Kenedy & Sons.

BROTHERHOOD OF ST. PAUL, THE. *The Clifton Tracts* (Library of Controversy). New York: P. J. Kenedy.

BUTLER, FRANCIS J. *Holy Family Catechism,* No. 3. Boston: Thomas J. Flynn & Co., 1904.

CATHOLIC ENCYCLOPEDIA, THE. New York: Robert Appleton Co., 1911.

CLOQUET, ABBE. *The Month of the Dead.* New York: Benziger Brothers, 1886.

CONVERT, H. *Eucharistic Meditations* (Extracts from the Writings of the Blessed J. M. Vianney). New York: Benziger Brothers, 1923.

CONWAY, BERTRAND L. *The Question-Box Answers.* New York: The Paulist Press, 1920. *Idem.* New edition. New York: The Paulist Press, 1929.

DEHARBE, JOSEPH, S. J. *A Complete Catechism of the Catholic Religion.* 6th American edition. New York: Schwartz, Kirwin & Fauss, 1924.

DOWLING, JOHN. *The History of Romanism.* 7th edition. New York City: Edward Walker, 1845.

DOYLE, Wm. *Shall I Be a Priest?* 16th edition. Dublin: Office of the Irish Messenger, 1936.

EDGAR, SAMUEL. *The Variations of Popery.* 10th complete American ed. New York: S. W. Benedict, 1850.

FERRARIS. *Lucius, Prompta Bibliotheca.* Venice, Italy: Gaspar Storti, 1772.

GEIERMANN, P. *The Convert's Catechism of Catholic Doctrine.* 1930. Reprint, Brushton, New York: TEACH Services Inc., 1995.

GIBBONS, CARDINAL JAMES. *The Faith of Our Fathers.* 110th Rev. ed. Baltimore: John Murphy Co.

HISLOP, ALEXANDER. *The Two Babylons.* 1905. Reprint, Brushton: TEACH Services, Inc., 2002.

KEENAN, STEPHEN. *A Doctrinal Catechism.* New York: P. J. Kenedy & Sons.

LABBE, PHILIPPE, and GABRIEL COSSART. *Sacrosancta Concilia.* France: Typographical Society, 1672.

LEO XIII. Encyclical letter The Reunion of Christendom, of June 20, 1894. See *The Great Encyclical Letters of Leo XIII.* 3rd ed. New York: Benziger Brothers, 1903.)

LIGHTFOOT, J. B. *Saint Paul's Epistle to the Philippians.* Rev. text. New York: Macmillan & Company, 1894.)

LIGUORI, ALFONSUS M. DE. *The Glories of Mary.* Rev. by Robert A. Coffin. London: Burns, Oates & Washbourne Ltd., 1868.

LOWELL, JAMES RUSSELL. "The Present Crisis." In *The Poetical Works of James Russell Lowell.* Household ed. Boston: Houghton Mifflin Co., 1916, 6.

MACEACHEN RODERICK. *Complete Catechism of Christian Doctrine.* Rev. ed. Wheeling: Catholic Book Co., 1911.

MARTIN, CHARLES A. *Catholic Religion.* Popular ed. St. Louis: B. Herder Book Co., 1919.

Bibliography

MOTH, EDWARD. "My Hope Is Built on Nothing Less." See hymn No. 522 in *Seventh-day Adventist Hymnal*. Washington, D. C.: Review & Herald Publishing Assn., 1985.

MULLER, MICHAEL. *The Catholic Priest*. Baltimore: Kreuzer Brothers, 1876.

MUZZARELLI, ESTHER. *Month of Mary*. London, Eng.: Burns and Oates, 1849.

———. *New Testament* (Roman Catholic translation). "A revision of the Challoner-Rheims version, edited by [Roman] Catholic scholars under the patronage of the Episcopal Committee of the Confraternity of Christian Doctrine." Paterson: St. Anthony Guild Press, 1941.

SEGUR, MGR., *Plain Talk about the Protestantism of Today*. Boston: T. B. Noonan & Co., 1868.

SMITH, WILLIAM, *A Dictionary of the Bible*. New York: Fleming H. Revell Co.

WATTS, ISAAC. "When I Survey the Wondrous Cross." See hymn No. 154 in *Seventh-day Adventist Hymnal*. Washington, D. C.: Review & Herald Publishing Assn., 1985.

WISEMAN, CARDINAL NICHOLAS. *Lectures on the Principal Doctrines and Practices of the Catholic Church*. Baltimore: J. Murphy, 1846.

PERIODICALS

Catholic Mind, The. (Jan., 1944).

Catholic Mirror, The, (Sept. 23, 1893).

Jesuit Seminary News, The. 3:9 (Nov. 15, 1928).

Kansas Catholic, The. (February 9, 1893).

Post-Standard, The. (Mar. 14, 1912).

Western Watchman, The, (Dec. 24, 1908; Dec.16, 1909).

We'd love to have you download our catalog of
titles we publish at:

www.TEACHServices.com

or write or email us your thoughts,
reactions, or criticism about this
or any other book we publish at:

TEACH Services, Inc.
254 Donovan Road
Brushton, NY 12916

info@TEACHServices.com

or you may call us at:

518/358-3494